Machine Q...

decorative threads

Maurine Noble &
Elizabeth Hendricks

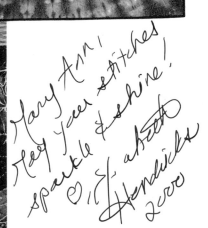

Mary Ann,
May your stitches
sparkle & shine!
♡ Elizabeth
Hendricks
2000

That Patchwork Place®

An Imprint of Martingale & Company

Credits

Editor-in-Chief	Kerry I. Smith
Technical Editor	Ursula Reikes
Managing Editor	Judy Petry
Copy Editor	Tina Cook
Proofreader	Leslie Phillips
Design Director	Cheryl Stevenson
Cover Designer	Margrit Baurecht
Text Designer	Kay Green
Design Assistant	Marijane E. Figg
Illustrator	Robin Strobel
Photographer	Brent Kane

Machine Quilting with Decorative Threads
© 1998 by Maurine Noble and Elizabeth Hendricks
Martingale & Company
PO Box 118
Bothell, WA 98041-0118 USA

Printed in Hong Kong
03 02 01 00 99 98   6 5 4 3

Title page:
GLOBAL WARMER by Maurine Roy, 1997, Edmonds, Washington, 41" x 41".

Free-motion stitched with flat polyester film through the needle.

Dedication

To my husband, Ed; my children—Lee, Elin and her husband Ron, Russ and his wife Diana; and my beautiful grandsons, Taylor and Adam. Thanks for your love and encouragement.

Maurine

To my husband, Kern, with thanks for your wit, wisdom, and wonderful support.

Elizabeth

Acknowledgments

Our thanks to the following needle and thread suppliers for the information and samples they so kindly shared with us: American & Efird Inc. (Mettler and Signature); Coats and Clark; Euro-Notions; Gütermann of America; Kreinik Mfg. Co., Inc.; Madeira West; Rainbow Gallery; Salus Textile; Sew-Art International; Sulky of America; and YLI Corporation.

A special thank-you to the quilt artists who generously allowed us to photograph and represent their work.

And thanks to Martingale & Company, for their help and support, and especially to Ursula Reikes, who held our hands during the development of this book.

> ### MISSION STATEMENT
>
> We are dedicated to providing quality products and service by working together to inspire creativity and to enrich the lives we touch.

Library of Congress Cataloging-in-Publication Data
Noble, Maurine
   Machine quilting with decorative threads / Maurine Noble & Elizabeth Hendricks
      p. cm.
   ISBN 1-56477-216-0
   1. Machine quilting. I. Hendricks, Elizabeth. II. Title.
TT835.H444 1998   97-44178
746.46—dc21   CIP

Contents

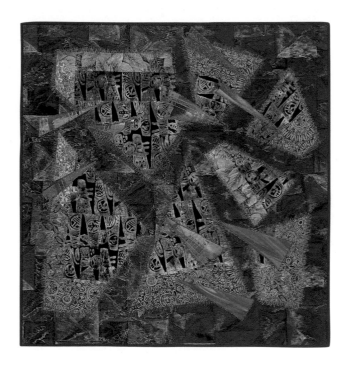

GYROSCOPIC PRECESSION by Elizabeth Hendricks, 1994, Seattle, Washington, 36" x 37".
  Free-motion stitched with flat polyester film and with metallic and rayon threads through the needle. Couched metallic yarns.

About the Authors

This book grew out of a friendship that began when Elizabeth took her first machine quilting class from Maurine in 1992. Since then, the two have shared their passion for beautiful threads. For Maurine, *Machine Quilting with Decorative Threads* is a natural extension of her first book, *Machine Quilting Made Easy*. For Elizabeth, this book is an outgrowth of her enthusiasm for using a wide variety of threads and styles of stitching in her art quilts.

Maurine Leander Noble has a degree in home economics education from Oregon State University. She taught clothing construction and machine-arts classes for fifteen years before finding the joy of machine quilting. A lifelong love of sewing machines has always challenged her to machine stitch what is usually done by hand. She now teaches machine quilting and appliqué classes nationwide. Maurine lives in Seattle, Washington, with her husband, Ed.

Elizabeth Purser Hendricks has a degree in fine arts from San Jose State University. She wrote the first documentary book on the Northwest wine industry, *The Winemakers of the Pacific Northwest* (Harbor House, 1977), and had an extensive career in the wine industry before discovering quilting in 1991. Her expressive art quilts have won numerous regional and national awards and have toured internationally. Her work has appeared in *Art/Quilt Magazine, Quilter's Newsletter Magazine, American Quilter Magazine, Quilter's Gallery,* and in more than a dozen books, including *Fiberarts Design Book Five*. Elizabeth teaches machine quilting and embellishment. She divides her time between homes in Seattle, Washington, and Central Oregon with her husband, Kern.

DETAIL OF SPARKLE PLENTY, by Elizabeth Hendricks and Maurine Noble

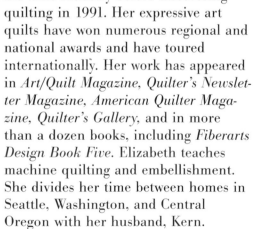

MAURINE AND ELIZABETH

Introduction

The threads you can use for machine quilting are as varied as the fabrics. If you haven't tried decorative threads, a whole new world of fun and excitement awaits you. If you have tried decorative threads and struggled with some of them, the hints and hands-on exercises in this book will solve many of your difficulties.

We start with a discussion of the basic supplies and techniques necessary for successful machine quilting. The remainder of the book consists of exercises divided in two sections. The first five exercises deal with threads that are used in the needle of the sewing machine. Exercises six through eleven cover threads that must be used in the bobbin or couched on the surface of your quilt. Each exercise addresses threads that require the same or similar handling.

Our goal was to illustrate how you can successfully use decorative threads in your quilting projects and to share our experiences with you. Once you've understood, practiced, and mastered the machine-quilting process, you'll be able to use any thread you find.

Use this book as a workbook. Write notes in it to remind you of successful and not-so-successful thread combinations. When you complete an exercise, you can make it into a pillow top as a reminder of your success.

While it's impossible to name every thread on the market, we've attempted to cover those most readily available and those you can order from catalogs. Brand availability differs from area to area, so first try those you can buy locally; sewing-machine dealers will most likely offer the best variety. You may also find unexpected treasures in needlework, knitting, and weaving shops. After experimenting with the threads available in your area, expand to mail-order suppliers (see "Resources" on page 84).

We want you to have as much fun planning and executing your machine quilting as you do designing and piecing your quilt top. As you learn to respect the abilities of your machine, it will become a good friend. Have fun playing with decorative threads, but be careful—it can be addictive.

Note: For basic quilting procedures, like layering and securing your quilt in preparation for machine quilting and attaching binding, refer to Maurine's first book, *Machine Quilting Made Easy.*

DETAIL OF GYROSCOPIC PRECESSION
by Elizabeth Hendricks

Getting Started

There are a few tools and techniques you will want to be familiar with to make machine quilting easy and enjoyable.

Sewing Machine

Knowing your sewing machine is essential to your machine-quilting success. Some older machines may have difficulty accommodating some decorative threads. Each machine has unique traits, and you should understand and feel comfortable with yours.

If you're in the market for a new sewing machine, think about how you plan to use it. If you want to free-motion quilt, take a quilt sandwich (quilt top, batting, and backing) with you when machine shopping and go through the process of changing from a walking foot to a darning foot. Stitch on your sample with each of the feet. You'll change presser feet many times while quilting a project, so it's good to compare different machines for ease of use. Be sure to test the machine's ability to adjust the length and width of all its stitches, noting how easy it is to do. Computer technology lets you tell the machine if you want it to stop with the needle up or down, how many times you want a pattern to repeat, if you want the pattern to stitch in a mirror image, and much more.

VEST by Melody Johnson, 1995, Cary, Illinois.
Bobbin quilted with hand-dyed pearl cottons.

The thread-tension dial on your machine has a number that indicates the normal setting, with additional numbers higher and lower than normal so you can tighten or loosen the top-thread tension. When you use decorative threads, you'll need to adjust the tension. The normal-tension number will vary with each machine, with each thread used, and with various bobbin-case adjustments. For some decorative threads, it isn't unusual to have a balanced tension when the dial reads a very low number. Disregard the number on the dial, but look for a balanced stitch on both the front and back of your quilt.

TIP: When you unthread your machine, cut the thread at the top of the machine, pull the spool up and off the spindle, and ease the cut length of thread down through the threading path and needle. This way, you won't compress lint in the tension disc by pulling thread the wrong way through the disc.

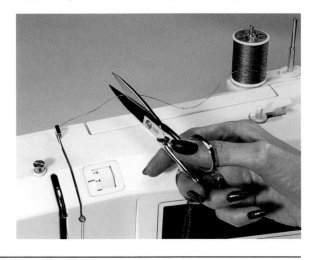

Walking Foot

The walking foot (also called the even-feed foot or Dual Feed) prevents layers from shifting while you stitch on a quilt sandwich. A regular presser foot pushes the top layer of the quilt forward as you stitch, creating tucks and distorting the shape of the quilt. Use a walking foot when stitching in-the-ditch or along straight lines or gentle curves, and when applying binding.

Walking feet are available for almost all machines. If there's a walking foot designed for your machine, use it; if not, generic walking feet are available. See your sewing-machine dealer for help in selecting a walking foot for your machine.

Darning Foot

The darning foot allows you to stitch in any direction without turning the fabric. It's possible to quilt circles, feathered wreaths, waves, floral motifs, and many other patterns once you're comfortable with free-motion stitching.

The darning foot has a hopper action that causes the foot to move up and down when the machine is stitching, thus allowing room for you to move the fabric. Darning feet vary in design with each brand. Some manufacturers make a darning foot that is open in front for better visibility. If an open-front darning foot is not available for your machine, you can have the front cut out—see your sewing-machine dealer.

When free-motion stitching with a darning foot, you need to drop or cover the feed dogs. Some older machines don't allow you to drop or cover the feed dogs. In this case, set the stitch length to 0, or to the shortest stitch, and ignore the feed dogs. Some machines have a dial on the left side of the machine head or a post at the top left of the machine that releases pressure on the presser foot. On a few older machines, there is a knob that needs to be set to the darning symbol. Your machine manual will tell you how to set up your machine for free-motion stitching with a darning foot.

Second Bobbin Case

If you plan to use heavy decorative threads, you'll need to wind them on the bobbin rather than run them through the needle. For this, you should have a second bobbin case. Use the extra case for threads that are lighter or heavier than normal; reserve your regular bobbin case for normal-weight threads. To identify the second case, dot it with nail polish.

Needle Basics

Selecting the correct needle is an important part of successful machine quilting. There are many types of needles available, and most of them have been developed with a specific purpose in mind.

Needle sizes are indicated by two numbers, for example 80/12 and 90/14. The first number is the European size, and the second number is the American size. The lower the numbers, the finer the needle.

Two categories of needles that are most useful for machine quilting are Sharp needles with normal-size eyes and Sharp needles with larger eyes. Sharp-Microtex, Jeans/Denim, and Quilting needles are all Sharp needles with normal-size eyes. Each has a sharp point that penetrates multiple layers without flexing to make a straight, clean stitch.

Embroidery needles have a large eye and a deep scarf (groove). The point is flexible, which helps when you're stitching a build-up of thread, as with free-motion machine embroidery. The Embroidery needle is a good choice for rayon, Neon, silk, and smooth, lightweight metallic threads.

Needles made especially for metallic threads are Metafil by Lammertz, Metallica by Schmetz, and Madeira Metallic. These are all the same type of needle and are referred to as *Metallic* needles in this book. Metallic needles have an even larger eye, which allows the rougher and more fragile metallic threads to slide through easily. They are available in sizes 70/10, 80/12, and 90/14.

When none of the previously mentioned large-eye needles prove successful, try a Topstitch needle. It has the largest available needle eye and a deep scarf, which makes it the perfect needle for heavy or textured threads. We recommend keeping a package of 90/14 Topstitch needles on hand for threads that shred when used with other needles.

Needles don't stay sharp forever. Sewing with decorative threads, particularly metallic ones, will wear your needle. The life of a needle is determined by the amount of stitching done and the contents of the quilt sandwich. The sharp point dulls faster when you're stitching through polyester or cotton-polyester batting than when you're stitching through all-cotton batting. If you have any of the following problems while stitching, change your needle.

- **Small strands of batting on the quilt back.** Bearding on the quilt back occurs most often when the needle dulls and punches strands of batting through the backing.

- **Noisy stitching.** A dull needle makes a thumping sound, and if the point of the needle is damaged, you will hear and feel the change.

- **Skipped stitches.** Skipping usually means the needle is dull or damaged or that the needle is inserted incorrectly in the machine.

- **Shredded top thread.** Change the needle as soon as a metallic thread begins to shred or break. The abrasive thread can damage the needle eye, and the damaged needle will contribute to the splitting and shredding of the thread.

When choosing a needle for each decorative thread, consider the thread size and texture. If the needle is too small for the thread, the thread will fray and eventually break. If the needle is too large for the thread, the stitching will be unattractive, with visible needle holes. In the charts on pages 78–83, we give needle suggestions for specific threads. If more than one needle is listed, try the one listed first (the finest one). If the thread shreds, breaks, or doesn't stitch well, try the next one on the list. Do this until you find the needle that works best for your quilt sandwich, thread, and machine. When you understand the criteria, it's easy to decide which needle type and size to try.

Marking Your Quilt Top

There are a number of ways to mark a design for quilting. You can mark the whole quilt top at once, which is tedious, or you can mark each area as you are ready to stitch it. We have a few other methods for you to consider.

≈ Cut a simple pattern from Con-Tact paper. Place the sticky side of the pattern on the quilt top or back, stitch around it, remove the Con-Tact pattern, then place it on the next area to be quilted.

≈ For a single image, trace the desired pattern with a fine-line permanent marker on lightweight tracing paper or doctors' exam-table paper. Pin the paper in place on your quilt and stitch through the paper. Remove the paper carefully, gently pulling it away from the stitching.

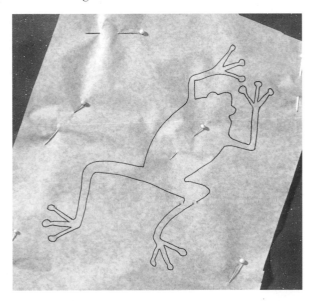

≈ For multiple, identical images, begin with a pattern stencil or a traced pattern. On a copy machine, enlarge or reduce the pattern to fit the space on your quilt. Using lightweight tracing paper or doctors' exam-table paper, cut paper to the desired size and layer the number of sheets needed, placing the photocopy on top of the pile. Insert a used needle (it can be dull) in your sewing machine. With a darning foot on the machine and no thread, free-motion stitch the pattern to perforate the paper layers. You can easily stitch through twenty to twenty-five sheets of tracing or exam-table paper with a used 90/14 Topstitch needle.

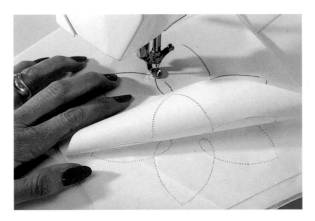

Pin each pattern in place on the quilt top or back. Change to a new needle, select your thread, adjust the tension, and free-motion stitch the pattern, using the perforations as a guide. If your pattern is symmetrical, stitch from the back of the perforated paper; the holes are easier to see. If your pattern is asymmetrical, however, stitching from the back will result in a reversed image.

TIP: When you change the needle in your machine, put the discarded needle in a plastic film container. You'll have used needles handy when you want to make perforated-paper patterns.

≋ If it's difficult for you to see the line on a perforated pattern, draw the design on tracing paper with a transfer pen or pencil. Lay the traced design facedown on another piece of tracing paper and press with a hot iron. One tracing will make up to ten copies. Do not transfer the pattern to the fabric—it's permanent and will never wash out. Remove the paper pattern immediately after stitching—the color from the transferred line will discolor the thread if left for a long period.

≋ Use a ruler and a Hera marker to mark straight lines. The marker makes a crease in the fabric that will remain until you stitch over it, spray it with water and press dry with an iron, or wash the quilt.

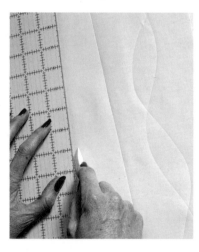

≋ Mark lines with a chalk wheel. Since the chalk disappears with handling, mark only a few lines at a time. Use white chalk on colored fabrics; colored chalk may not come out.

≋ Use a washable pen to draw a quilting pattern on your fabric. Following a stencil or traced pattern, mark lightly, making a dotted line instead of a solid one. Don't expose the quilt to direct sunlight or heat, because this will set the marks. To remove the marks after stitching, immerse the quilt in cold water, then wash with mild soap in a washing machine on gentle cycle. Laundering ensures that the chemical from the marking pen is removed from the fabric and batting.

≋ Use quilters' pencils, which come in white, yellow, and silver, to trace or draw a pattern on your fabric. If marked lightly, they can be washed out.

Free-Motion Stitching

While a lot can be done with a walking foot, the freedom of drawing spontaneously on a quilt can only be achieved with free-motion stitching. If you've never done free-motion stitching or if you haven't practiced for a while, we recommend that you run through the following steps to warm up.

1. Sandwich a 14" square of lightweight batting between two 14" squares of solid fabric. Safety-pin baste.
2. Insert a new 80/12 Sharp or Denim needle or a 75/11 Quilting needle in your sewing machine.
3. Thread the machine and fill the bobbin with lightweight cotton thread.
4. Drop or cover the feed dogs. Release pressure on the presser foot if necessary.
5. Attach a darning foot.
6. If your machine allows, adjust the speed to one-third or one-half, and set the needle stop to the down position.
7. Place the quilt sandwich under the darning foot, then lower the presser foot.

8. While holding the top thread, rotate the flywheel toward you one complete rotation until the take-up lever is in its highest position. Pull the top thread to bring the bobbin thread up. You'll see a loop on top of the quilt sandwich.

9. Move the quilt sandwich to one side of the needle. Pull the top and bobbin threads where they loop together to bring the top thread down through the darning foot and the bobbin thread up through the fabric. The two threads should be under the darning foot. Move the quilt sandwich back in position.

10. To secure the ends, hold the thread tails while running the machine and slowly moving the fabric forward about ⅛". This will create very small stitches at the beginning of your stitching. Cut off the thread tails.

11. If you are able to decrease the speed of your machine, do it, then floor the foot pedal while stitching and moving the fabric. It's easier to develop a rhythm with a limited machine speed. If you don't have speed control, don't floor the foot pedal—the machine will go too fast at first. To run at a lower speed, apply less than full pressure to the foot control.

    Concentrate on the movement of the fabric, trying to make the stitches as even as possible. The faster you move the fabric, the longer the stitches; the slower you move the fabric, the shorter the stitches.

12. To secure the end of a line of stitching, run the machine and slowly move the fabric forward about ⅛" to make very small stitches. Cut off the thread tails.

Tips for Free-Motion Stitching

Try to maintain an even speed and a controlled motion. You'll feel out of control at first, but you'll develop confidence with practice.

Without turning the quilt sandwich, stitch while moving it backward, forward, and sideways. Stitch in a circular motion and in a triangular motion. Make wiggly lines and write your name. Think of the stitching as continuous doodling, as if the needle were a pencil and the quilt a piece of paper. Stitch in this manner until you feel comfortable and have reasonable control. If you have trouble controlling the movement of the fabric, there are several aids that may help.

❧ Wear cotton garden gloves or cotton-knit quilters' gloves with small rubber dots on the palms; they will help you grab the fabric.

≋ Try rubber file fingers or finger cots.

≋ Try a "half-a-hoop" to stabilize and move the fabric. This idea is from Denise Schultz. You can make a half-a-hoop by applying ¼" strips of Dr. Scholl's Foot and Shoe Padding (an adhesive-backed foam) to the top or bottom of one ring of a 6" machine-embroidery hoop. A machine-embroidery hoop is narrower than a hand-embroidery hoop and will slide easily under the darning foot. If you can't slide the hoop under the needle and darning foot of your machine, apply the foot and shoe padding to the outer ring of the machine-embroidery hoop. Remove the screw and gently open the hoop, spreading it around the needle and darning foot. Lift and move the hoop as necessary while stitching.

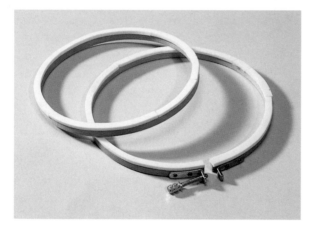

Suggestions for Machine Quilting

≋ Remove your shoes. You'll be able to control the speed much better when stitching in your stocking feet.

≋ Play music so you have a beat or rhythm to stitch by.

≋ Set a timer to thirty minutes. Every thirty minutes, take a break and do a few exercises to loosen up and get your blood circulating before returning to your machine.

Testing the Tension

We recommend you do a tension test for each combination of top and bobbin thread you intend to use.

1. Using a permanent pen, mark a 14" square of fabric with horizontal lines at 2" intervals, or use a 14" square of Creative Grid.

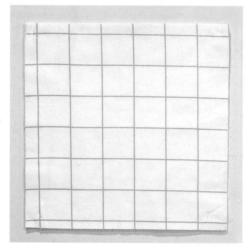

Creative Grid

2. In the left margin, mark the center line with the number that corresponds to normal tension on your sewing machine (5 is usual). Mark the two lines above the centerline with the next two lower numbers (4 and 3) and the two lines below the centerline with the next two higher numbers (6 and 7).

3. At the top of the fabric, write the names and weights of the top and bobbin threads, and the needle size and type you are testing. Also note any stitch information (length and width, stitch number).

4. Make a quilt sandwich by layering the marked fabric with batting and backing fabric. Baste the layers together with safety pins.

Tip: With adhesive basting spray, you can prepare a quilt for quilting in a fraction of the time that pinning or tacking requires. Try it on a small project first, following the directions on the can. Use the adhesive spray outside or in a well-ventilated room.

---

5. Prepare the machine with needle, thread, and walking foot (feed dogs up), and select a stitch to test.

6. Set the tension to the lowest number marked on your test fabric. Set the straight-stitch length at 4 to 5mm (5 to 8 stitches per inch), and stitch from the first to the second line. Stop, increase the tension to the next higher number, and stitch from the second line to the third line. Continue in this manner, working your way through the tension numbers on your test fabric. Repeat, using a zigzag stitch (width 4 or 5, length 4).

7. Look at the top and back of the quilt sand-wich to determine which tension number results in the best looking and most balanced stitch. Circle that section on the front of the test fabric. If it's difficult to see differences in the tension from number to number, look at how the thread lies on the top. If it's too loose, the top thread may pull to the back. If it's too tight, the stitching line will look strained and puckered, and the top thread may pull the bobbin thread to the top. It's easier to see the changes in tension in the zigzag stitch. You may have to renumber your test fabric in smaller increments (3, 3½, 4, 4½) to get a balanced stitch.

8. Repeat the same test with a darning foot (feed dogs down or covered). Always stitch your tension sampler the way you intend to stitch your quilt (if you want to stitch spirals on your quilt, stitch spirals on your tension sampler). The best tension may be different from the one you found with a walking foot. Circle the balanced-tension area.

If the marked tension numbers don't produce a balanced stitch, adjust the numbers until the stitches balance. Don't be alarmed if you have a balanced stitch at a number that is a long way from the normal setting; it could even be 0. The fabric and batting, the weights of the top and bobbin threads, and the bobbin-case tension adjustment all affect the top tension.

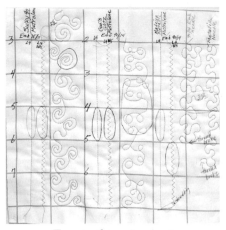

Front of tension test.

Back of tension test.

The tension test gives you a starting point. Once you've chosen the thread and corresponding needle for your project, we recommend that you stitch a tension test on the fabric and batting you plan to use. Begin with the balanced tension setting from your original test and proceed from there. You may find that the same thread stitched on a different quilt sandwich requires a slightly different tension adjustment.

TIP: Sewers Aid is a lubricant that stabilizes thread, but use it with caution. Some people are sensitive to the chemical it contains. If you use the correct needle for each thread, adjust the thread tension, and stitch evenly and slowly, you may not need to use a thread lubricant.

Threads Through the Needle

The first five exercises deal with threads that can be successfully stitched through the needle of a sewing machine. Each exercise lists a group of threads with similar characteristics. You'll get the best results when you use the correct needle, bobbin thread, and tension setting. Do a tension test before you begin each exercise to make sure you have a balanced stitch.

When machine quilting with decorative threads, you need to choose colors that will show against the fabrics in your quilt top. A close color match is good for cotton thread that you want to blend with the fabric, but not good for a rayon or metallic—if decorative threads don't show, there's no need to use them. Choose a thread that matches the color of the fabric but is lighter or darker, or try a contrasting color or a variegated thread. Play with thread on swatches of the quilt-top fabric until you find a color that shows up against and enhances the fabric. When selecting thread, consider how it will appear when stitched into your quilt and how easy it is to use with your machine.

The numbering system for thread weight is the reverse of numbering for needle size. A low number means thick thread and a high number means fine thread. The ply is the number of twisted strands that are again twisted together to form the finished thread. The number 50/3 on a thread spool indicates 50-weight and 3-ply. When only one number is printed on the spool, such as 30 or 40, you can assume the thread is 2-ply.

Note: If you have problems using thread in the needle, you can wind that thread on a bobbin, adjust your bobbin-case tension, and stitch from the back of your quilt. See "Threads from the Bobbin" on page 40.

Tip: Store thread away from direct sunlight, and cover it with a cloth to keep it dust-free. A closed plastic bag doesn't let the thread breathe; it's better to store thread in a drawer or on a covered shelf.

For best results, the thread in the bobbin needs to correspond with the thread in the needle. It should be approximately the same weight as the top thread, or at least strong enough to support it. If appropriate, you can use the top thread in the bobbin as well. Don't use metallic thread in the bobbin unless you're stitching a reversible quilt—metallic threads are abrasive and tend to cut each other when used in the top and in the bobbin. Bobbin-thread suggestions are included in the thread charts and are listed for each exercise.

Bobbin threads

There are several brands of threads that are intended for bobbin use with lingerie and machine embroidery. We refer to these as *bobbin threads* in this book. They are made from nylon or polyester and are fine in weight and very strong. Bobbin threads work well with lightweight metallic and rayon threads. They can also be used through the needle for fine, almost invisible stitching. Mettler Metrolene is the only one that comes in colors other than black and white.

Tip: Use caution when winding a bobbin with monofilament or bobbin thread. Run the machine at a slower speed and fill the bobbin only three-quarters full. Plastic bobbins require special care. If you wind the bobbin too fast, the thread can build up and cause the bobbin to swell, which will cause problems when you stitch. In some cases, the bobbin will wind unevenly, pop open, or tighten on the bobbin spindle so it can't be removed.

You can also buy bobbins prewound with white machine-embroidery bobbin thread that fit class 15 bobbin cases. This is a handy way to purchase bobbin thread. Test the prewound bobbins in your machine, using various types of decorative thread in the needle, to see if you can control the tension and whether you like the results. We have had varying degrees of success with prewound bobbins.

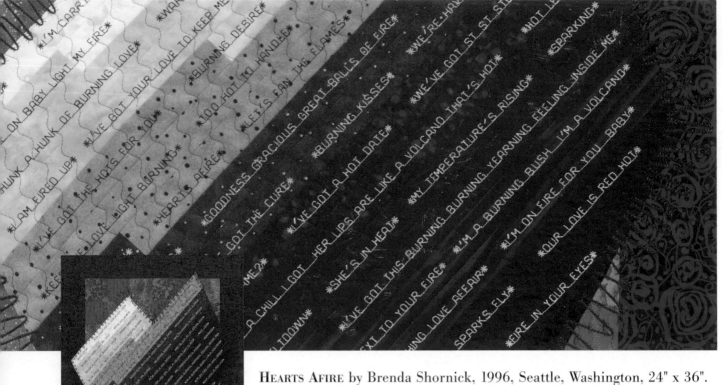

HEARTS AFIRE by Brenda Shornick, 1996, Seattle, Washington, 24" x 36".
Programmed lettering stitched with rayon thread; RibbonFloss couched around heart's edge with metallic thread.

DETAIL OF NIGHT BLOOMS, pieced by Sue Linker and quilted by Judy Axlund, 1997, Enumclaw, Washington, 72" x 72".

Free-motion stitched with variegated rayon thread through the needle.

MINIATURE #114 by Caryl Bryer Fallert, 1997, Oswego, Illinois, 14" x 19".
Free-motion stitched with 30-weight variegated cotton through the needle.

THREE BUTTERFLIES by Elizabeth Hendricks,
1993, Seattle, Washington, 50" x 39".
(Collection of John and Denise Hendricks.)
*Free-motion stitched with textured metallic
thread through the needle.*

**DETAIL OF WHERE'S
WALDO AND HIS TWO
KITES?** by Becky Hansen,
1993, Mukilteo, Washing-
ton, 76" x 58".
*Free-motion stitched
with opalescent Madeira
Supertwist through the
needle.*

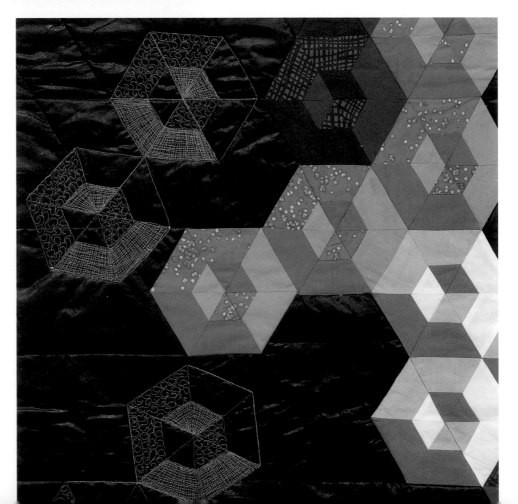

SERENITY by DuAnn Wright, 1996, Meridian, Idaho,
45" x 59".

*Free-motion stitched with tatting cotton and rayon
threads through the needle; zigzag-stitched bark.*

GEOMETRY IN THE FIELDS
by Heather W. Tewell, 1997,
Anacortes, Washington,
61" x 42".
   Free-motion stitched with 50-weight cotton through the needle.

HOLLYHOCKS II by Melody
Johnson, 1997, Cary, Illinois,
57" x 40½".
   Free-motion stitched with hand-dyed #12 pearl cotton through the needle.

ZELL AND CLAY'S MAGICAL LILY POND by Sonia Grasvik, 1997, Seattle, Washington, 14½" x 14½" x 2¾".

Free-motion stitched with iridescent textured metallic threads through the needle.

DETAIL OF AMISH TRIP AROUND THE WORLD by DuAnn Wright, Meridian, Idaho, 1994, 52" x 52".

Flat polyester film stitched through a twin needle with a walking foot.

REFLECTION by Elizabeth Hendricks, 1996, Seattle, Washington, 41" x 44".
Free-motion stitched with 100-weight machine-embroidery cotton through the needle.

PANEL VEST by Judy Bishop, 1997, Carson, California.
Custom programmed stitches done with Cotty cotton thread.

REHEARSAL by Janet Steadman, 1996, Clinton, Washington, 49" x 50".
Variegated rayon stitched through the needle with a walking foot.

DETAIL OF CHAIN OF ROSES by Becky Hansen, 1997, Mukilteo, Washington, 43" x 60".
Roses and stippling stitched free-motion with rayon thread; variegated rayon stitched through a twin needle with a walking foot.

Cotton and Transparent Monofilament Threads

$\mathcal{C}$otton threads are the easiest threads to use for machine quilting and are the best choice for bed quilts. For dense or traditional quilting, it's advantageous to use a fine, lightweight thread that will sink into the surface of the quilt. DMC 50, Madeira Cotona 80, Mettler 60/2 machine embroidery, and Coats embroidery Dual Duty are considered lightweight cotton threads. These threads are not strong, so it's best to use them for background quilting like stippling. Use a stronger, more durable thread to stitch in-the-ditch when anchoring or stabilizing your quilt.

Mettler Silk Finish Cotton, Coats Dual Duty Cotton, and Gütermann Cotton are slightly heavier than the threads previously mentioned, and therefore stronger. They are good choices for general piecing as well as for stitching in-the-ditch on a bed quilt that will get daily use and frequent washings. But they are not so heavy that they look like rope lying on the surface of the quilt, nor are they so strong and abrasive that they could damage cotton fabric.

Transparent monofilament thread comes in polyester and nylon. It disappears against the quilt surface, but it does have a slight sheen that can give a quilt an undesirable plastic appearance. Monofilament thread is nice for stitching on multicolored fabrics or around a multicolored appliqué. We do not recommend using monofilament thread on quilts meant for infants or young children.

There are so many variables that it can be difficult to choose threads, but the deciding factor must be the ultimate use of the quilt and the desired appearance. A wall hanging doesn't need to withstand heavy use, so the threads can be very different from those you might use on a bed quilt.

Exercise 1
Background Stitches

$\mathscr{I}$f you've never done free-motion quilting before, or if it's been a while since you did, we recommend you do the exercise that starts on page 10. When you feel comfortable with free-motion stitching, it's time to try some traditional and nontraditional fill-in stitches like stippling, spirals, and geometric continuous patterns.

SETUP CHART	
Top thread	Your choice of lightweight cotton or monofilament
Bobbin thread	Same as top in weight and color
Needle	To match thread weight
Top tension	Normal for cotton thread, slightly loosened for monofilament thread
Stitch	Straight
Stitch length	N/A
Stitch width	0
Foot	Darning (feed dogs down)

1. Prepare a 20" x 20" quilt sandwich.
2. Thread the needle and insert the bobbin with the appropriate thread combination. Test the tension on scraps of fabric and batting.
3. With a fine-line permanent pen, trace the design (page 85) onto lightweight tracing paper or doctors' exam-table paper. Pin the pattern to the center of the quilt sandwich and remove pins or tacks from under the paper.
4. Free-motion stitch the continuous pattern. Carefully remove the paper.
5. With a Hera marker and ruler, score lines to divide the remainder of the piece into 10 sections as shown. Stitch the scored lines, using a walking foot (feed dogs up). Check the stitching every once in a while to see if the tension looks balanced on both the top and back sides.

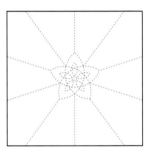

6. Attach a darning foot, drop the feed dogs, and fill in the sections with some of the continuous patterns shown below and on page 26, or make up your own.

≋ Loops can be fat and round or skinny and long. Be sure to vary the direction in which you stitch them.

❧ Spirals can be any shape: round, triangular, oval, or square. When stitching the inward path of a spiral, be sure to allow enough space between lines so that you can stitch your way out. Stitch in a continuous motion, and don't tie off in the center of the spiral. You can later fill in between the lines if space allows.

❧ Stippling looks like the knobs of a jigsaw-puzzle piece repeated over and over without crossing previously stitched lines. The knobs can be round, long, regular or irregular, and any scale desired. Each quilter develops her own brand of stippling.

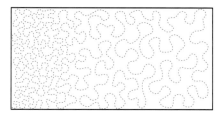

❧ Combined elements, such as stars or spirals with stippling, can be nice.

❧ Peacock feathers are fun. Begin with a teardrop and outline the original shape a few times; repeat. Give the end of the teardrop a slight point to turn it into a leaf.

❧ Echo quilting radiates from a central design. Start by following the outer line of the central pattern, then repeat.

❧ Stone (repeated circles of various sizes) and trailing leaf patterns are also great background designs.

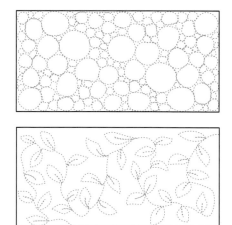

Rayon, Silk, and Neon Threads

𝓡ayon threads are user-friendly and have a subtle sheen. The most readily available brands are Sulky, Madeira, and Coats. Sulky doesn't print the word "rayon" on the spool, but it's recognizable by the sheen. Rayon is available in 30 and 40 weights. When stitched, 30-weight thread makes a thicker, more obvious line than 40-weight.

Coats Color Twist is a 35-weight twisted rayon thread that combines two colors for an unusual heathered look. With variegated rayons, the stitching seems to appear and disappear on the quilt surface as the thread progresses from one color to another. When satin stitched, variegated rayons create blocks of color as the hue changes.

Sulky and Madeira also make many colors of ombré thread—a gradation of values of one color. Madeira's 30-weight variegated rayon looks like hand-painted splotches of color. Both of these variegated threads blend with multicolored fabrics and are especially effective on watercolor quilts.

Rayon thread doesn't wear as well as strong cotton thread. It should be used alternately with a cotton thread for a bed quilt destined to get lots of use. Use strong cotton thread to anchor or stabilize a quilt, then use rayon thread to embellish the surface.

Silk threads have an elegant luster and are strong and easy to use, but they are pricey. Madeira makes an eye-catching polyester thread called Neon. Its distinctive luminous look is perfect for highlighting areas you want to pop out. Both silk and Neon threads behave like rayons and should be treated the same way.

Tip: The stretch, triple, and long stitches don't work well with a walking foot. You can get much better stitch quality with a general-purpose foot. However, you may need to help the quilt sandwich along as it goes under the foot. With the index fingers of both hands on either side of the front edge of the presser foot, gently push the fabric toward the foot as the machine stitches.

SETUP CHART	
Top thread	Variegated rayon
Bobbin thread	Same as top, 50/3 cotton, or polyester or nylon bobbin thread
Needle	75/11 or 90/14 Embroidery
Top tension	Normal or slightly loosened
Stitch	Decorative double or triple, or straight
Stitch length	Lengthen for decorative, 4mm to 6mm for straight
Stitch width	Default for decorative, 0 for straight
Foot	General sewing foot or walking foot*

*Try each foot to see if there is a difference in stitch quality.

1. Thread the machine with variegated rayon thread.
2. Choose a straight stretch-stitch and lengthen it. Stitch a straight line on the second third of your sampler.

3. Change to a triple zigzag stitch, changing the straight stretch-stitch to the widest setting; stitch another line. The sampler on page 29 shows both normal and stretched straight and zigzag stitches.
4. Choose another double or triple stitch, such as a feather stitch or blanket stitch. Stitch as many as you can find on your machine.
5. Stitch a few simple decorative stitches, lengthening the stitch of each slightly.
6. Attach a darning foot and stitch a free-motion design.
7. Tie off the ends as described in the Tip on page 29.

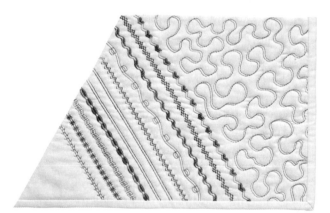

Exercise 2C
Twin-Needle Stitching

𝒯win needles come in a variety of needle types and sizes. There are two numbers on the needle case. The first is the distance between the needles (for example, 2.0 means 2mm apart), and second is the size of the needles. We prefer Metallic twin needles, size 2.0/80 to 3.0/80, because the needles are a bit stronger than Embroidery twin needles and don't break as easily. This type of needle is friendly to fragile threads.

Because there is just one bobbin thread, it will always make a zigzag on the back of the quilt to catch both top threads. The farther apart the needles, the wider the zigzag on the back. Use a lightweight cotton or bobbin thread for less bulk.

Tip: Make a habit of having at least two sets of twin needles on hand when you are quilting a project, just in case you break one.

Twin-needle stitching can be used for straight lines or gentle curves, for programmed decorative stitches or for free-motion stitching. When using decorative stitches, be sure to adjust the stitch width to accommodate the width of the needles. Some computer sewing machines have a twin-needle control button that limits the stitch width. Always double-check this by turning the hand wheel through one sequence of the stitches that make up the decorative stitch. If the stitch width is set too wide, the needle will hit the foot as it swings to the extreme right or left. If necessary, decrease the stitch width to prevent a broken needle.

Tip: If the maximum stitch width of your machine is 5mm and the twin-needle width is 2mm, set the stitch width no wider than 3mm. (Maximum stitch width minus twin-needle width = maximum width setting: 5 − 2 = 3).

Use two equal-sized spools of same-weight thread to balance the pull of the thread through the tension discs (right spool clockwise, left spool counterclockwise). To thread the machine, separate the threads, placing one on each side of the tension disc, then together through the remainder of the thread guides. This keeps the threads from twisting and eventually fraying and breaking. If the threads fray and break, loosen the tension and don't pass the threads through the last guide before threading the needles. It's important to run your machine at a slow but steady speed. No flooring the foot control!

SETUP CHART	
Top threads	Two spools of rayon of the same spool size, weight, and brand; solid color and variegated
Bobbin thread	Polyester or nylon bobbin thread
Needle	Twin Embroidery, or twin Metallic
Top tension	Slightly looser than normal
Stitch	Decorative, straight, or free-motion
Stitch width	Maximum stitch width minus needle width for decorative, 0 for straight and free-motion
Stitch length	Lengthen decorative, 4mm to 6mm for straight, N/A for free-motion
Foot	Walking for straight and decorative stitches (feed dogs up); darning for free-motion (feed dogs down)

1. Insert the twin needle and thread your machine.
2. Attach the walking foot. Choose a simple programmed decorative stitch, such as a feather stitch.
3. Adjust the stitch width to allow for the swing of the needle; use the twin-needle safety button if you have one. If you can, set the machine to one-third or one-half speed.
4. Test the tension on scraps of fabric and batting. It's okay if you see some rayon thread on the back side.
5. Stitch on the last third of your sample. Remember to check the tension on the top and back sides of the quilt sandwich. You should see a bit of the top thread on the back side.
6. Try a lengthened straight or zigzag stretch-stitch if you have these options on your machine. Each line of stitching will look like three strands of thread rather than one. Continue with other simple decorative stitches.
7. Remove the walking foot and attach a darning foot. Drop or cover the feed dogs.
8. Free-motion stitch, running the machine at a moderate speed. When you stipple in a large, circular motion, the two threads create a ribbonlike pattern. Play with some of the patterns you practiced in Exercise 1 (pages 25–26).

Lightweight Metallic Threads

Lightweight metallic threads can add sparkle and elegance when used sparingly, or they can make a quilt sing when used heavily and playfully. They are attractive stitched in a single line and in programmed decorative stitches, and they look great in satin stitching, background stitching, and free-motion stitching. Outlining a fabric motif with metallic thread is an easy and attractive way to enhance your quilt.

Metallic threads are fragile and don't wear well on bed quilts that get heavy use. They are more appropriate for wall quilts.

Working with metallic threads can be challenging, but your skills will increase as you practice. Each brand is slightly different, and some are easier to use than others. The most readily available brands of light-weight metallic threads are Sulky, Madeira, YLI, Kreinik, Signature, Gütermann, and Coats. Each has a slightly different look and weight and has its own unique appearance when stitched.

Because metallic threads fray and break easily, you must always do a tension test (page 12). When you find an unfamiliar brand, buy it and test it.

SPARKLE PLENTY, pieced by Elizabeth Hendricks and quilted by Maurine Noble, 1996, Seattle, Washington, 33" x 33".

Free-motion stitched with Madeira Supertwist metallic thread through the needle.

Metafil, Metallica, and Madeira Metallic 70/10, 80/12, and 90/14 needles work well with most metallic threads. A very lightweight metallic thread, such as Kreinik Cord or YLI fine metallic, often stitches well with a 75/11 or 90/14 Embroidery needle.

The weight of metallic thread is not always printed on the spool; however, you can see and feel weight differences. Pull a strand of thread between your thumb and forefinger to determine which needle will be appropriate. If the strand feels bumpy or rough, you need a Metallic or Topstitch needle. The top thread slides in and out of the needle eye many times during stitching, so some metallic threads fray and break if the needle eye is too small. The larger eye of a Topstitch needle may help.

If a metallic thread continues to cause problems, try loosening the tension and using a 90/14 Topstitch needle. If the thread continues to break after you change to a larger-eyed needle, carefully wind the thread on a bobbin and stitch backing side up. See "Threads from the Bobbin" on pages 40–64.

It's not a good idea to use metallic thread in the bobbin when you have metallic thread in the needle, because metallic threads have a tendency to cut each other. When used in the bobbin, cotton machine-embroidery thread is also easily shredded by abrasive metallic threads. We recommend using a polyester or nylon bobbin thread.

Tip: Use a needle threader with decorative threads, especially with metallic threads that separate immediately after cutting.

Exercise 3
Feathered Heart and Grid Background

For this exercise, try your hand at stitching a traditional feather.

SETUP CHART	
Top thread	Your choice of lightweight metallic
Bobbin thread	Polyester or nylon bobbin thread
Needle	70/10, 80/12, or 90/14 Metallic or 80/12 or 90/14 Topstitch
Top tension	Normal with walking foot, slightly loosened with darning foot
Stitch	Straight
Stitch length	3mm
Stitch width	0
Foot	Walking for straight (feed dogs up); darning for free-motion (feed dogs down)

1. Prepare an 18" x 18" quilt sandwich.
2. Attach a walking foot. On scraps of fabric sandwiched with batting, stitch a long straight stitch (3mm) to determine the correct tension. If the thread repeatedly shreds and breaks, try the next-largest needle and loosen the top tension.

3. Remove the walking foot and attach a darning foot. Test the tension again. You may need to loosen the top tension slightly.

4. With a fine-line permanent pen, trace the feathered heart (page 86) onto lightweight tracing paper or doctors' exam-table paper.

5. Center the pattern on the quilt sandwich and pin it in place.

6. Stitch through the paper, on the lines—but do not stitch the centerline yet. Tie off when beginning and ending the design (page 29).

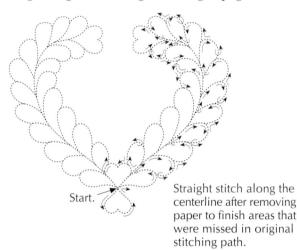

Start.

Straight stitch along the centerline after removing paper to finish areas that were missed in original stitching path.

7. Trim the thread tails and gently pull the paper away from the stitches. You may have to scratch lightly with your fingernail to remove small pieces trapped under the double stitching. If the paper is difficult to remove, the remaining small pieces will wash out.

8. Stitch the centerline of the feathered heart, then stitch the background grid. Beginning ⅛" from the starting point, reverse six to eight stitches with a short straight stitch (.05mm). Stitch forward over the small reverse tie-off stitches with a longer quilting stitch (length 2.75 or 3mm), continuing to the end of that row. Repeat the tie-off at the beginning and end of each row.

Background Stitching Options

≈ Mark the grid lines with a ruler and a Hera marker or chalk wheel (see page 10).

≈ Using a Hera marker or chalk wheel, mark one line to use as a starting point. Stitch on the marked line. Stitch the other grid lines by aligning the edge of the walking foot with the line just stitched (you can change the needle position to make narrower or wider spaces between grid lines).

≈ If you have an extension-arm guide on your walking foot, you can use it to control the width of the rows.

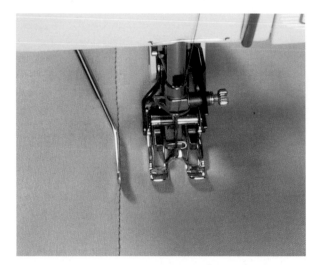

≈ To stitch the grid in the center of the wreath, lay a sheet of paper along the pattern, connecting the background grid lines on either side of the wreath; pin in place. Stitch, using the edge of the paper as a guide for your first line, then align the edge of the walking foot or the arm guide with previous stitching to complete the grid.

Tip: If you have a computerized machine that recalls stitch alterations, set the straight-stitch length at 2.75mm for the quilting stitch. For a tie-off stitch, set the zigzag stitch at 0 width and between .05 and .025 length. You can then switch between the tie-off stitch and the straight stitch as needed for each row. The machine will remember these alterations until you turn it off.

Flat Polyester Film

Several manufacturers produce a thin, flat, ribbonlike polyester film that is coated with aluminum. Because the flat film catches and reflects light, it produces a showy and sparkly line of stitching. These are sometimes called "Mylar threads" or "tinsel threads." Sulky's version is called Sliver and Coats's is Glitz. Jewel by Madeira and Glissen Gloss Prizm Hologram are similar, but they have a faceted look. Hologram threads come in only six colors, while Sliver and Glitz are available in a wider color range, including some iridescent colors.

The thread spool needs to be placed in a vertical position on the machine. Flat-film thread tends to twist as it unwinds from the spool and runs through the tension discs and thread path of the sewing machine. When the twists tighten in the tension discs, the thread breaks.

Stitch slowly, adjusting the tension as needed. With flat-film thread, free-motion stitching usually requires a looser top tension than straight stitching with a walking foot. Use a 90/14 Embroidery needle. If this doesn't work, try a 70/10, 80/12, or 90/14 Metallic needle.

Flat film is also attractive in a decorative stitch. Use a walking foot and keep the stitch simple, lengthening it just a bit. Flat film isn't as pretty in satin stitching; because the film twists during stitching, it doesn't fill a satin stitch evenly.

If you want a glitzy look, flat film is the best choice. It's great for holiday stitching, or wherever more is better. David Walker has a saying he shares with his classes, which is well suited to flat polyester-film thread: "Excess is never enough."

Note: Flat-film thread works better on some sewing machines than others. If you have insurmountable problems using this thread in the needle, try it in the bobbin. Because less strain is put on the thread when it is pulled from the bobbin, there is less twisting, so the thread doesn't break or shred as easily. See "Threads from the Bobbin" on pages 40–64.

1. Prepare an 18" x 18" quilt sandwich.
2. Test the tension on scraps of fabric and batting.
3. Using a permanent pen, trace the frog (page 86) onto lightweight tracing paper or doctors' exam-table paper. Make 3 patterns.
4. Pin the paper patterns to the quilt sandwich and free-motion stitch the designs. Carefully tear away the paper.
5. Free-motion stitch inside the frogs, using patterns from Exercise 1. Stitch other shapes in the background, such as lily pads and watery lines. Experiment with different colors and brands of flat-film thread, including the hologram varieties.

SETUP CHART	
Top thread	Any flat-film thread
Bobbin thread	Polyester or nylon bobbin thread
Needle	70/10, 80/12, or 90/14 Metallica or 90/14 Embroidery
Top tension	Slightly looser than normal
Stitch	Straight
Stitch length	N/A
Stitch width	0
Foot	Darning (feed dogs down)

Heavy Threads

*T*here are several heavy threads that you can stitch through the needle of a sewing machine. Madeira Cordonnet, YLI Jeanstitch, and Gütermann Topstitching threads are polyester threads that resemble buttonhole twist. They are often referred to as "topstitching threads." Madeira Burmi-Lana, Gunold Stickma Luny, and Sew-Art Renaissance are combinations of 30% wool and 70% acrylic.

Pearl cottons in sizes 12 and 8, Caron Wildflowers, Gunold Stickma Cotty, and various tatting and crochet cottons are all heavy cotton threads. When stitched, these threads create a thick, dominant line, which resembles Japanese sashiko quilting.

Pearl cotton comes in a wound ball or twisted skein. A ball will feed from a vertical spool pin or thread stand, but watch carefully so the thread doesn't wind around the spool pin.

Twisted skeins need to be wound on a spool before you can use the thread on a machine. You can wind the thread onto a spool by hand, or you can use an EZ Winder (available in most sewing-machine stores), which attaches to the sewing machine's bobbin winder.

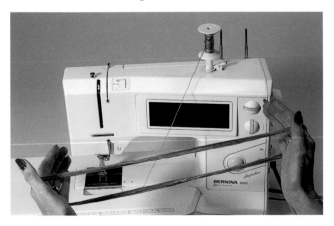

Note: Hand-quilting thread is also considered a heavy thread, but we don't recommend those with a waxed finish for machine quilting. The glazed or waxed finish on many quilting threads is not good for tension discs, and waxed thread stitches a heavy, stiff, thready-looking line.

When using heavy threads through the needle, use a bobbin thread of equal weight. We often use the same thread for both the top and the bobbin, or we switch to 30-weight cotton thread for the bobbin. Use your second bobbin case, adjusting the tension to accommodate the heavy thread (see pages 46–47).

For successful results with heavy threads, it's important to stitch slowly and use a simple stitch.

For Japanese sashiko-style quilting, use any of the heavier threads. Use the same brand and weight of thread in the bobbin and through the needle. Match the bobbin-thread color to the background fabric, and choose a contrasting color for the top thread. Traditionally, the top thread is white and the bobbin thread is navy blue, with the stitching done on indigo fabric. Loosen the bobbin tension and tighten the top tension to expose the bobbin thread between each stitch. Use a long stitch so that it resembles a hand stitch.

Exercise 5
Free-Motion Borders

Stitched with YLI Jeanstitch variegated thread.

SETUP CHART	
Top thread	Your choice of topstitching thread
Bobbin Thread	Same as top thread or 30-weight cotton
Needle	90/14 Topstitch
Top tension	Normal or slightly tighter
Stitch	Straight
Stitch length	N/A
Stitch width	0
Foot	Walking for straight stitch (feed dogs up); darning for free-motion (feed dogs down)

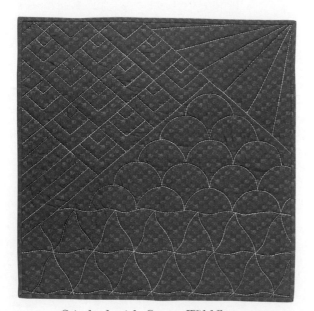

Stitched with Caron Wildflower variegated thread.

1. Piece a simple 18" x 18" quilt top as shown below. Use a printed fabric for the middle and a solid for the large border sections. Layer the top with batting and backing.

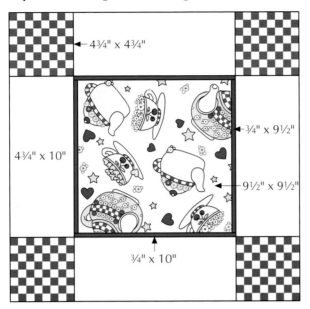

2. Using a walking foot, stitch in-the-ditch along the seams. Use a matching-color lightweight cotton thread or a monofilament thread.
3. Remove the walking foot and attach a darning foot. Thread the machine with appropriate topstitching and bobbin threads. Remember to change the needle to match the topstitching thread.
4. Test the tension on scraps of fabric and batting, beginning with the top tension at normal setting. If you start with the tension too loose, the threads will jam in the machine when you begin to stitch. You'll probably have to increase the thread tension by one or two numbers.

5. Free-motion quilt in the wide borders. You can stitch one pattern in all the borders, or try a different pattern on each side.
6. Make another 18" x 18" quilt sandwich. Trace the rope border (page 88) and stitch, using a walking foot with feed dogs up, and a feather stitch or other simple programmed stitch. A loose zigzag looks nice.

   We made the sample by first stitching over a paper pattern with a long straight stitch, using invisible monofilament thread in the needle and bobbin. We removed the paper, then stitched over the monofilament thread line, this time using a programmed feather stitch with #12 pearl cotton and a 90/14 Embroidery needle. It would have been difficult to remove the paper if we'd done the feather stitching on it.

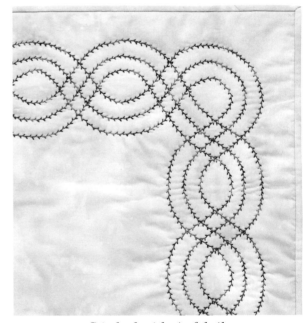

Stitched with Artfabrik variegated #12 pearl cotton.

Threads from the Bobbin

Bobbin quilting is a versatile way to incorporate decorative threads, braids, and ribbons into your quilting or surface embellishment. Many threads are too large or oddly shaped to fit through a needle or too delicate to withstand the tension action when stitched from the top. Because threads on the bobbin unwind slowly and pass through the bobbin's tension spring, they are not subjected to the stress and wear experienced by threads on top.

To bobbin quilt, you stitch with the quilt top facing down, so that the "top" thread in the needle (what you see while quilting) shows on the backing and the bobbin thread shows on the front. We recommend taking longer stitches at a slower speed while bobbin quilting. Long stitches show off decorative threads better.

Whenever an asymmetrical design is stitched from the back side, it will produce a mirror-image design on the front.

CRAZY ROSE by Laura Wasilowski, 1994, Elgin, Illinois, 40½" x 34".
Bobbin quilted with hand-dyed pearl cotton.

BASKING IN THE LIMELIGHT by Libby Lehman, 1997, Houston, Texas, 57" x 57".
Lightweight metallics stitched through the needle; bobbin quilting and couching.

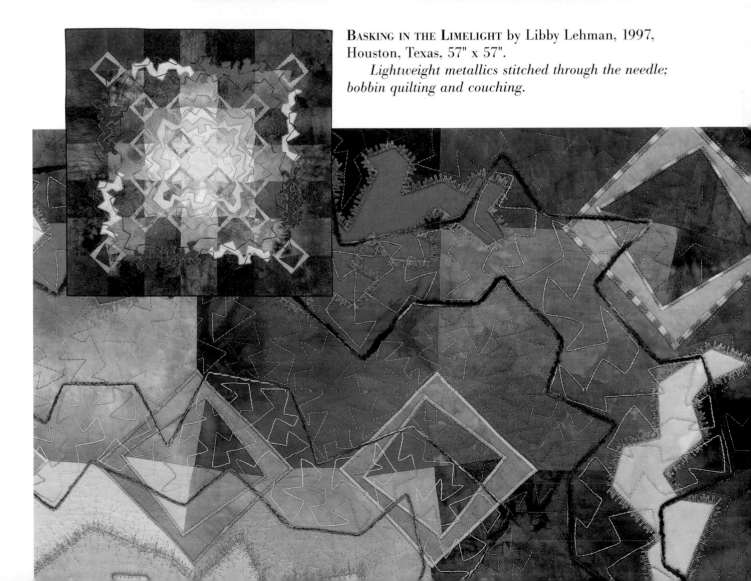

Inside   *Outside*

Silk vest panel by Vickie Hu Poirier, 1997, Las Cruces, New Mexico.
    Bobbin quilted with metallic threads, cable, and braids from the inside of the vest panel, over a design printed on commercial fabric; the design appears as a mirror image on the outside.

UNSPOKEN TEARS by Elizabeth Hendricks,
1994, Seattle, Washington, 42" x 63".
(Collection of Julie and Kim Rackley.)
   Detail shows bobbin-quilted RibbonFloss.

SASHIKO DRESS by Melody Johnson, 1992,
Cary, Illinois.
   Bobbin quilted with pearl crown rayon.

LATTE by Elizabeth Hendricks, 1995, Seattle, Washington, 18½" x 18½".
   Stitched with metallic threads through the needle; bobbin quilted with heavy metallic thread, metallic ribbon, and RibbonFloss. Couched metallic yarn, cotton chenille, and flat metallic braid.

MOCHA by Elizabeth Hendricks, 1995, Seattle, Washington, 18½" x 18½".
    Free-motion stitched with flat polyester film and with metallic and rayon threads through the needle. Bobbin quilted with heavy metallic thread and RibbonFloss. Couched metallic braid, metallic ribbon, metallic thread, and rayon braid. Hand-stitched beads. More than fifty different threads, braids, ribbons, and yarns were used in Mocha and in Latte on the facing page.

Bobbin-Quilting Basics

𝒲ind the bobbin. Thread the decorative thread from the inside, through a hole on the bobbin's side (see page 50). Machine wind the bobbin slowly, holding the loose thread tail long enough to secure the center with several layers of wound thread. Then snip off the tail, flush with the outside of the bobbin.

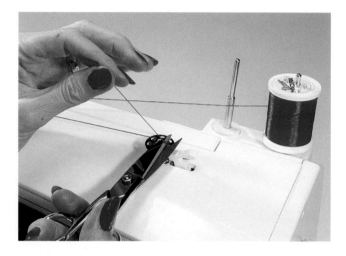

Tip: If your machine can't wind the bobbin slowly, hold your thumb on top of the bobbin as it winds, using pressure to slow the speed. Continue winding the bobbin until it's about three-quarters full.

Check the tension. Place the filled bobbin in your second bobbin case. Ease the decorative thread through the tension spring. If the thread is too thick to fit through the tension spring, loosen the bobbin tension before sliding the thread through the tension spring. If the thread is plied or woven, be careful that strands don't catch on the tension spring. Once the bobbin is loaded, pull out several inches of thread to make sure it glides freely.

Hold the decorative thread in one hand, suspending the bobbin case, with your other hand cupped six to eight inches below the hanging case. If the bobbin is so loose that it won't hang suspended, you need to tighten the bobbin tension.

Think of the screw on the bobbin case as the face of a clock. When adjusting, turn it in "five-minute" increments. Remember, left is loose and right is tight. With each small turn, check the tension by pulling on the thread. When the tension is tight enough that the bobbin will hang suspended, give a gentle jerk to the thread. If the bobbin drops slowly and requires several jerks to reach your hand, the tension is correct. If the bobbin case drops quickly into your hand, tighten the bobbin tension by turning the screw to the right in small increments.

Conversely, if the bobbin tension is so tight that the thread doesn't move, loosen the tension by turning the screw to the left in small increments. Be careful not to loosen the screw so much that it falls out and the tension spring loosens. (Some quilters loosen their bobbin cases over a folded towel or a bowl just in case.) If the screw falls out, collect it and the flat metal tension spring, and put the bobbin case back together.

You'll need to adjust the bobbin tension for each weight of thread, braid, or ribbon. Over time, you'll develop a feel for making adjustments.

Tip: If adjusting the tension causes a quantity of thread to unwind, remove the bobbin from its case and slowly rewind it on your bobbin winder. Replace the bobbin in its case, then test once more to confirm proper tension.

Load the bobbin case. If you have a drop-in bobbin (without a separate bobbin case), check the machine manual or see your dealer to learn how to make tension adjustments.

Select a top thread. You can choose a top thread that either blends or contrasts with the fiber content, color, and value of the decorative thread in the bobbin. Because bobbin quilting is done on the back, the top thread shows as little dots between each stitch on the front of your work. Strong rayon, metallic, and cotton threads can all be used on top. Each will produce a different effect. Make sure to match the machine's needle to the top-thread type and weight.

Adjust the stitch length. Decorative threads show better and stitch more easily in a long stitch length. If the maximum length on your machine is 4mm or 5mm, try the basting stitch.

Tighten the top-thread tension. A tight top tension compensates for the loose bobbin tension and creates a more attractive and secure stitch. If 5 is normal on your machine, tighten the tension toward 6.

Choose a presser foot. For straight-line or gently-curved stitching, use a walking foot, and make sure the machine's feed dogs are raised. For free-motion stitching, attach a darning foot and drop or cover the feed dogs.

Test the tension. Attach a walking foot, and rotate the needle once by hand to bring up the bobbin thread. Insert a 14" quilt sandwich, backing side up, under the presser foot. Make sure all the basting pins are on the quilt's back, so you see them on top of the work as you stitch. Lower the needle into the quilt by hand, then lower the foot. Stitch the length of the fabric. Snip the top and bobbin threads, turn your piece over, and evaluate the stitches. Referring to the chart below, make necessary adjustments and stitch another line. Continue adjusting the top and bottom tensions until you are pleased with the stitch appearance. Also critique the stitch length and top-thread compatibility.

APPEARANCE OF STITCHES	PROBLEM	SOLUTION
Stiff, straight	Bobbin tension too tight	Loosen bobbin tension screw (left)
Loopy, meanders left and right	Bobbin tension too loose	Tighten bobbin tension screw (right)
Lies on surface, not defined	Top tension too loose	Tighten top tension
Pulled too tight into quilt	Top tension too tight	Loosen top tension

Making First and Last Stitches

In bobbin quilting, the cleanest beginnings and endings are created by placing the first and last stitches by hand, once a line of quilting is completed.

1. Take the first stitch with the hand wheel. Insert the needle ⅛" or one stitch length from the starting point, leaving 4" tails. Once the needle is down, lower the presser foot. Place your hands securely on your work and begin stitching.

2. Stop stitching ⅛" or one stitch length from the point you want the line of stitching to end. Lift the presser foot and pull the top thread slack on your machine. Reach under (or pinch from the top) to hold the decorative thread in place on your work, then pull the quilt from the machine. Cut the top and bobbin threads, leaving 4" tails. This special care will help protect the even tension of your stitches. Otherwise, you run the risk of pulling the last few stitches too tightly. If this happens, carefully slide a straight pin under each stitch to slightly loosen the decorative-thread stitches, working from the center out.

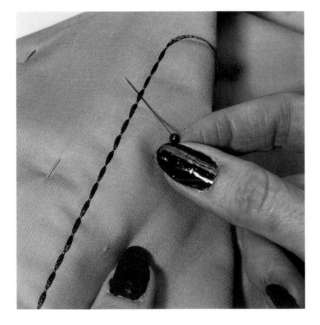

3. Thread the beginning or ending tail of the decorative thread onto a large-eyed hand needle. Decide where to take the first or last stitch, then poke the needle straight through to the back. Gently tug the hand stitch, so the tension is even with the machine stitches.

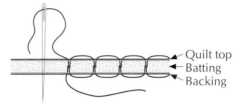

From the back, tie the tails of the top and bobbin threads in a square knot (right over left, then left over right).

Using a needle threader, thread both tails onto a large-eyed hand needle. Pierce the back of the quilt next to the knot at an angle. Run the needle through 1" to 1½" of the batting parallel to the backing, then out the back, without piercing the front. Gently tug on both thread tails to pull the knot into the batting. Cut the threads flush with the fabric.

Repeat this hand-stitch and tie-off procedure every time you begin or end a line of stitching. This method leaves a clean back, secures the threads, and keeps your quilting smooth.

Tip: Before removing a bobbin of decorative thread, cut the thread flush with the top of the bobbin case, then pull out the bobbin. Cutting the threads instead of pulling them backward through the tension discs helps preserve the tension spring.

To get a feel for bobbin quilting, quilt straight lines with a walking foot, then progress to free-motion quilting with a darning foot.

Many of the techniques in the following exercises can be done with a variety of decorative threads. Some of the more delicate threads, such as plied rayons, have less versatility. And some, such as RibbonFloss, require special care. The heavier decorative threads used in bobbin quilting can also be applied by couching (see pages 65–77).

Frog Frolic by Maurine Noble, 1997, Seattle, Washington, 42" x 52".
Free-motion bobbin quilted with #5 pearl crown rayon.

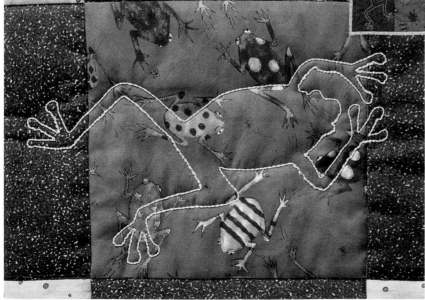

Plied Threads

$\mathcal{P}$lied threads are composed of a multitude of thin strands that are lightly twisted together. Plied rayon thread was originally developed for the serger. It has lovely shine, softness, and malleability. However, it's not as strong as other decorative threads and doesn't wear well, so you may want to use it only for decorative stitching on wall or art quilts.

Because of their loose construction, plied threads need special handling when it comes to winding the bobbin and loading the bobbin case. The ends of plied threads fray immediately when cut. To fill the bobbin, fold the thread in two. Pinch the fold to make a point, then thread it from inside the bobbin, out through the hole as shown below. Leave a 4" tail, then proceed to wind the bobbin slowly while holding the tail.

It's easiest to stitch plied threads in straight lines or gentle curves. They are temperamental when used for free-motion quilting, because they don't tolerate abrupt changes in direction. The fine strands tend to catch on the bobbin-tension hook when you change stitching direction, which then jams the bobbin mechanism.

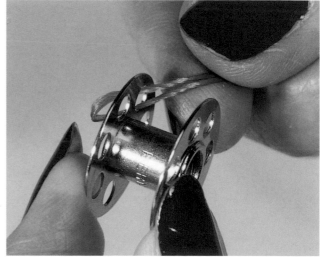

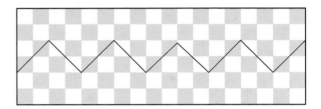

1. Make a 14" x 14" quilt sandwich, using a solid fabric for the top and a checked fabric for the backing. Pin-baste from the backing side.
2. Start on the left-hand side. Using the longest stitch length available, stitch the length of the quilt, following a line on the back fabric.
3. Stitch a second line with a medium-length stitch.
4. Turn the quilt over and compare the different stitch lengths. If the maximum stitch length on your machine is 4, you may not like the appearance of this thread. If you can make a longer basting stitch, stitch another line.
5. Using white, nonwaxed chalk, draw a zigzag pattern along the length of the backing, diagonally across the checks.

6. Stitch from the edge, following the chalk line. When you reach a corner, stop with the needle down, lift the walking foot, and pivot the quilt until the chalked line runs straight in front of the foot. Lower the foot, then stitch to the next corner and repeat the pivot. Continue along the length of the quilt.
7. Repeat steps 5 and 6 in a smaller zigzag.

*U*sing a walking foot is the most reliable way to quilt with plied threads. A checked backing fabric makes it easy to draw and stitch zigzags and geometric spirals.

SETUP CHART	
Bobbin thread	Plied rayon
Top thread	30- or 40-weight rayon, in color to match plied rayon
Needle	75/11 or 90/14 Embroidery
Top tension	Slightly tighter than normal
Second bobbin case	Adjusted to plied thread
Stitch	Straight
Length	Long
Stitch width	0
Speed	Slow
Foot	Walking (feed dogs up)
Quilt position	Backing side up

8. Draw a geometric spiral as shown. Follow the check to keep the lines straight and the corners square.

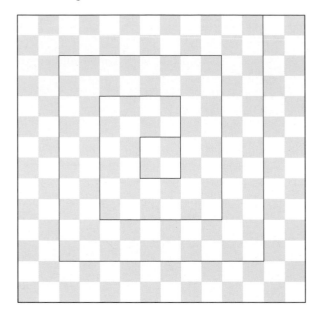

T<small>INDERBOX</small> by Libby Lehman, 1993, Houston, Texas, 46" x 46". (Collection of Maurine Noble.)
  Free-motion bobbin quilted with plied thread; free-motion stitched with metallic threads through the needle.

9. Stitch from the edge to the first corner and pivot with the needle down. Continue stitching and pivoting to the center.
10. Stop one stitch length from the end of the line. Take the last stitch with a hand needle, tie off, then bury the thread ends (see page 48).
11. Change bobbin thread colors and try more geometric designs, following the lines and squares of the check.

Tip: When stitching zigzags or geometric spirals, you may need to adjust the stitch length so it hits evenly at the pivot point. If the walking foot is in the middle of a stitch when you want to end a line of stitching, lift the walking foot and slowly move the quilt so the next stitch falls precisely at the turning point. Then adjust the stitch length so the next line of stitching ends at the pivot point.

Pearl Threads

$\mathscr{P}$earl threads include pearl crown rayon and pearl cotton. Pearl crown rayon is a smooth, lustrous twisted rayon that is easy to quilt with from the bobbin. This thread is round and soft. It is well-suited to free-motion curves and continuous-line designs because it doesn't tangle or snag on the bobbin-tension hook when you change stitching direction.

Pearl cotton has a matte finish and comes in a variety of weights. It wears better than pearl crown rayon and is a good embellishment thread for clothing.

Pearl threads look best in long stitches. They can also be used with some programmed decorative stitches; however, you may need to increase the stitch length to accommodate the thick thread. Use a walking foot for straight lines or gentle curves. For complex free-motion patterns and curvilinear lines, use a darning foot. If your machine has a basting stitch, use it to allow for a more relaxed rhythm while free-motion stitching.

SASHIKO SAMPLER II by Elizabeth Hendricks, 1997, Seattle, Washington, 22" x 20".
Bobbin quilted with variegated pearl crown rayon thread.

Exercise 7
Quilting a Mon Design

SETUP CHART	
Bobbin thread	Pearl crown rayon or pearl cotton
Top thread	30- or 40-weight rayon or 30-, 40-, or 50-weight cotton
Needle	75/11 or 90/14 Embroidery or 75/11 Quilting
Top tension	Slightly tighter than normal
Second bobbin case	Adjusted to pearl thread
Stitch	Straight
Stitch length	N/A
Stitch width	0
Speed	Slow
Foot	Darning (feed dogs down)
Quilt position	Backing side up

*I*n this exercise, you will stitch a design with many points and tight curves to show off the versatility of pearl threads. A mon design is a traditional Japanese family crest. Many such designs are copyright-free and can be found in a number of books. Before stitching a new pattern, practice tracing the design with your fingertip to familiarize yourself with it, and note any places where lines intersect. You can begin stitching at an intersection or at an inside point where a stop and start won't be noticed.

1. Prepare an 18" x 18" quilt sandwich (a checked backing fabric can help you keep the pattern aligned in step 3). Safety-pin baste from the backing side.
2. Using a permanent black pen, trace the mon design (page 87) onto lightweight tracing paper or doctors' exam-table paper.
3. Safety-pin the design in place on the backing. Check the pattern's alignment; you want it to be straight on the quilt.
4. Starting at a point inside the design, insert the needle on the black line, ⅛" or one stitch length from your starting point.
5. Stitch the design through the paper. Run the machine slowly and move the quilt at a regular pace to keep the stitches even. This takes a little practice. Stitch smoothly around each outside point rather than stopping and starting at the point. If you need to readjust your hands, stop at an inside point on the design or along a straight area, where it's easier to restart without interrupting the flow of the line.
6. Stop one stitch length or less from the end.
7. Carefully remove your quilt, then take the first and last stitches by hand. Tie off, then bury the thread ends (see page 48).
8. Carefully tear away the paper by pulling it sideways from the stitches.

Metallic Braids

*R*ound metallic braids are wonderful for bobbin quilting. They behave much like pearl threads but add sparkle to your work. Our favorite round metallic braids are made by Kreinik. Kreinik braids are made for both hand and machine stitching and can be found in craft, needlework, and fabric stores.

Kreinik makes three thicknesses of metallic braid. The Medium #16 and Fine #32 braids both work well in the bobbin. The Heavy #8 is too large to fit through a bobbin. We recommend couching #8 with metallic thread (see pages 65–77).

Kreinik braid can be bobbin quilted in a classic sashiko pattern for a contemporary look. Sashiko is a traditional Japanese hand-quilting method, in which a long running stitch of heavy cotton thread is made through several layers of cotton fabric.

Tip: If you want to embellish a vest, jacket lapel, or other wearable with metallic braid, begin with a rectangle 2" larger than the pattern on all sides. After the bobbin quilting is complete, lay the pattern (right side up) over the quilted rectangle and outline the pattern with chalk. Stitch ¼" inside the chalked line all the way around. This stay stitching will hold the braids in place while you cut out the pattern pieces.

Exercise 8
Quilting Sashiko Style

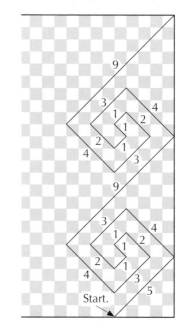

$\mathcal{W}$e chose the simple Inazuma, or lightning, pattern for this exercise because it can be stitched in a continuous line, edge to edge. This design has 90° corners, although 60° is traditional. To get accustomed to stitching straight lines in many directions without turning your quilt, try this pattern free-motion. If free-motion stitching is too difficult at first, use a walking foot with feed dogs up. Use a checked fabric for the backing, with ½" to ¾" squares, so you can keep track of the pattern.

SETUP CHART	
Bobbin thread	Medium- or light-weight Kreinik Metallic Braid
Top thread	Smooth metallic (not nubby or wound on a polyester core)
Needle	80/12 Metallic
Top tension	Tighter than normal
Second bobbin case	Adjust to metallic braid
Stitch	Straight or a basting stitch if your machine has one
Stitch length	N/A
Stitch width	0
Speed	Slow
Foot	Darning (feed dogs down)
Quilt position	Backing side up

1. Prepare an 18" x 18" quilt sandwich, using a checked fabric for the backing. Safety-pin baste on the backing side.
2. Using a chalk wheel and starting at the lower edge, draw a diagonal line on the checked fabric, five squares long, at a 45° angle. Make a 90° turn to the left. Draw a geometric spiral in a continuous line, using the checks as guides: 4-3-2-1-1-1-2-3-4-9 as shown below. Draw the pattern repeat to the opposite edge. To keep from getting lost in the pattern, count the number of checks you cross as you chalk and later stitch through the sequence.

3. Begin stitching across the first five diagonal squares. When you reach the corner, stop with the needle down. Stopping at the corner keeps the angle crisp.
4. Without turning the quilt, stitch across the four diagonal squares to the left. Try to move smoothly, so your stitches are even.
5. Continue stitching along the lines, pausing at each corner before changing directions. Stitch to the opposite edge, leaving a 2" to 4" tail.
6. Turn your quilt over to admire your lightning bolt. If the bobbin thread pulls in at the corners and the braid doesn't form crisp angles, tighten the top-thread tension slightly.
7. At the quilt's edges, tie the top and bobbin threads around the braid at each tail to hold it securely.

8. For fun, draw additional lightning bolts, nesting the patterns. Stitch in different colors of braid. While this is not traditional for sashiko, it can create a pleasing effect.

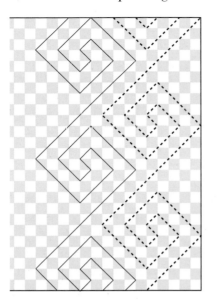

Note: When partial spirals form at edges, stitch in from the sides, and remember to leave tails. When stitching a garment piece, cut the tails off only after staystitching around the pattern piece or attaching the binding so the braid is always held securely.

Tip: If the bobbin runs out mid-pattern, remove the quilt from the machine and carefully lift out stitches from the backing side to a corner in the design. Begin the new bobbin at that corner, and take the first and last stitches by hand. Tie off and bury the threads and braids. The change should not be visible.

SASHIKO SAMPLER by Elizabeth Hendricks, 1995, Seattle, Washington, 18½" x 18½".
Bobbin quilted with RibbonFloss, heavy metallic thread, metallic filament, metallic braid, #7 Japan thread, and plied rayon.

Decorative Metallic Threads

*D*ecorative metallic threads offer sparkle and verve. They are a combination of metallic threads and other fibers that give them body, strength, and softness. Decorative metallic threads offer quilters an array of textures and effects. Since the various threads differ in fiber content, thickness, suppleness, and finish, you need to test each individually before quilting with it.

To test a decorative metallic thread, first stitch straight lines with a walking foot, adjusting the tension so each stitch is uniform. Next, stitch a geometric pattern, pivoting with the needle down at each corner. If the geometric pattern is successful, try free-motion stitching with a darning foot. First stitch gentle curves. If the thread tolerates this, try circles, then a design with tight curves and points. Stitching in this progression will show you the limits and possibilities of each decorative metallic thread. Because of the different thicknesses and fiber contents, you'll need to adjust the bobbin tension for each thread.

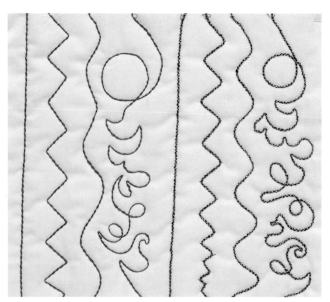

The ¹/₁₆" flat metallic ribbon at left stitched straight lines, pivots, and curves well. The acrylic-metallic braid at right was too bulky to pivot sharply and buckled when stitched free-motion.

To anticipate how a metallic thread will behave in the bobbin, the best thing to do is to feel it. Unwind 6" of thread and run your thumb and forefinger down its length. Notice if it's smooth or rough, soft or stiff, wiry or pliable. Then note if the thread is tightly twisted or braided, or if individual strands or filaments are loose along the edges. Lastly, try to pinch the thread into a point.

Soft threads, such as YLI Candlelight, Madeira Decor, and Kreinik Ombre, stitch smoothly through the bobbin. Their softness lets them easily stitch curves and points. Their thickness causes them to scallop slightly, so they look best in a uniform stitch length.

Very smooth, round threads, such as Madeira Metallic No. 6, Kreinik Japan thread, and Kreinik Cable, are less sensitive to variable stitch length. Their slight stiffness causes them to round tight curves smoothly. However, the thick Japan thread #7 might twist or buckle on sharp points. If you can't easily fold a thread into a point, use it for curvilinear designs rather than for patterns with sharp points.

Very rough metallics, such as Sew Art Flash and Radiance, can be sensitive to tension settings, because they snag easily on the bobbin tension hook. Approach them with caution.

Decorative threads with multiple loose strands, such as DMC Metallic Embroidery floss, stitch smoothly through the bobbin. However, if a strand catches on the tension hook, it quickly tangles. A slow, steady stitching rhythm often prevents this problem.

Bobbin quilting allows you to create your own blend of threads, as long as they are wound on the bobbin as one and threaded through the tension disc together. Combining similar lightweight threads, such as different colors of Kreinik Blending Filaments, works well.

See the thread charts for specific information on individual threads. Then, as you discover and evaluate new threads, note their characteristics on the charts for reference.

Courage in Turquoise by Ann Fahl, 1992, Racine, Wisconsin, 52½" x 59". *Free-motion bobbin quilted with flat polyester film.*

**Exercise 9
Quilting Fabric Motifs**

𝒫rinted fabrics can be ready-made sources of quilting patterns. Look for a print with floating design elements, and use it for your backing. When you bobbin quilt around the designs, the decorative threads will show on the front.

SETUP CHART	
Bobbin thread	Decorative Metallic
Top thread	Smooth metallic
Needle	70/10, 80/12, or 90/14 Metallic or 75/11 Embroidery
Top tension	Tighter than normal
Second bobbin case	Adjust for each decorative metallic thread
Stitch	Straight, or a basting stitch if your machine has one
Stitch length	N/A
Stitch width	0
Speed	Slow
Foot	Darning (feed dogs down)
Quilt position	Backing side up

1. Prepare an 18" x 18" quilt sandwich, using a printed fabric for the backing. Safety-pin baste from the back.
2. Fill several bobbins three-quarters full with different metallic threads.
3. Trace each design on the printed fabric with your finger to mentally note the stitching direction.
4. Beginning at an inside point on the design, free-motion stitch around it. Use shorter stitches when going around sharp curves. After completing the design, cut the threads, leaving 4" tails.
5. Turn the quilt over to assess your work, then take the first and last stitches by hand. Tie off and bury the top and bobbin tails (see page 48).

6. Switch bobbins to try another decorative thread. Stitch around a design and tie off the tails as before. Stitch around the remaining designs, changing bobbin threads as desired.

Back

Front

7. If you want the bobbin-quilted designs to stand out even more, turn to the top side of the quilt, remove the pins from the back, and free-motion stitch between the shapes. Use a lightweight thread in the needle that matches the background color.

If there's a fabric motif on the quilt top that you'd like to bobbin quilt with decorative thread, stitch the design from the top with lightweight metallic or monofilament thread, using a polyester bobbin thread that contrasts in color and value with the backing fabric.

Stitched from top.   *Back*

Turn the quilt backing side up. Insert a decorative metallic thread in the bobbin and stitch over the design from the back. Presto—the design now appears on the quilt front in gorgeous decorative thread

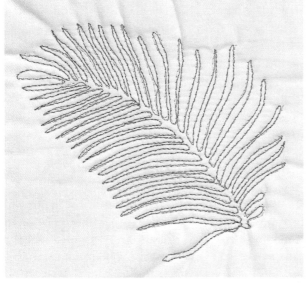

Stitched from back.   *Top*

Ribbons and Flat Braids

You can do all sorts of exciting bobbin quilting with flat RibbonFloss and silk ribbon. Ribbon's greatest strength, its flatness, makes it easy to wind on the bobbin. However, its flatness is also its greatest disadvantage. Should the ribbon twist while unwinding, it can quickly jam or snag on the hook of the bobbin-tension spring.

The versatility of metallic ribbons and flat braids depends on their thickness and stiffness. The narrower and softer, the easier to bobbin quilt. Frye Werks Needlepoint metallic ribbon and Kreinik Metallic Braid No. 4 are both narrow and supple enough to bobbin quilt free-motion. Madeira Metallic braid is too stiff to free-motion quilt and is best bobbin quilted with a walking foot in straight lines, programmed stitches, or gentle curves. Even stiffer and thicker metallic braids, such as Madeira Carat, won't stitch through the bobbin and should be couched.

RibbonFloss is reflective and lends a unique textural quality to quilting embellishment. Each stitch appears scalloped, because the top thread pulls in the sides of the ribbon. We recommend using a walking foot for straight, geometric, or gently curved designs. A uniform stitch length is important. Free-motion stitching can be done with a darning foot, but it takes practice to achieve consistent ribbon stitch length. RibbonFloss is particularly sensitive to tension settings. (See the problem-solving chart on page 47.)

Silk ribbon comes in luscious colors and has a matte finish. Ribbons up to 4mm wide can be bobbin quilted. Those about 2mm or 1/16" in width are the most versatile, because wider ribbons can buckle on sharp points or curves; wider ribbons are most successful when stitched in straight lines or gentle curves with a walking foot.

Exercise 10
Quilting Angles and Curves

SETUP CHART	
Bobbin thread	RibbonFloss or 2mm (¹/₁₆ ") silk ribbon
Top thread	40-weight rayon
Needle	75/11 Embroidery
Top tension	Tighter than normal
Second bobbin case	Adjusted to ribbon
Stitch	Straight
Stitch length	Long (6 to 8mm)
Stitch width	0
Speed	Slow
Foot	Walking (feed dogs up)
Quilt position	Backing side up

BOBBIN-WINDING RIBBONFLOSS

1. In front of your machine, place the ribbon tube on a spindle. This could be the knee-lift bar if your machine has one or a pencil with a wide eraser taped to the table.

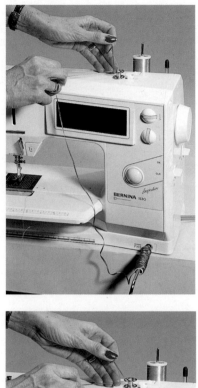

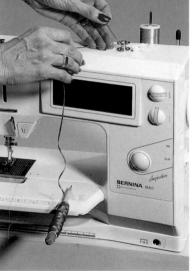

2. Keeping the ribbon flat, thread it onto the bobbin from the inside (see page 50). Place the bobbin on your machine.

3. Grip the ribbon tail on the bobbin with one hand. With the other, lightly hold the ribbon 3" to 5" from the bobbin to make sure the ribbon doesn't twist. Guide the ribbon so it stays flat and fills the bobbin evenly. Wind the bobbin only three-quarters full.

1. Prepare an 18" x 18" quilt sandwich, using a checked fabric for the backing. Pin-baste from the backing side.
2. Mark the quilt sandwich into 3 segments with chalk as shown, one for straight or border patterns, one for geometric shapes, and the third for random curved designs.

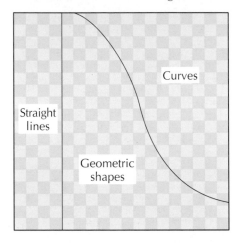

3. Start at the left edge. With the machine set at the longest stitch length, stitch a straight line from edge to edge. Follow the check pattern to keep the line straight. Using different ribbons for each, stitch two more straight lines about ¼" apart.
4. Switch to another ribbon and stitch two more straight lines, approximately 1½" apart.
5. Change the ribbon color again. Using a straight stitch, make a zigzag pattern between the last 2 lines you stitched. Stitch across the diagonal of the squares and pivot at the straight lines with the needle down. Adjust the stitch length, so the final stitch of each diagonal line is at the turning point.

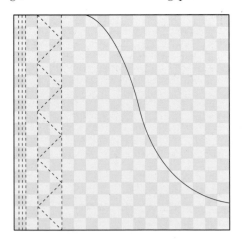

6. Stitch a second diagonal pattern, in the opposite direction, over the first. Where diagonal lines intersect, the stitches should cross each other without one piercing the other.

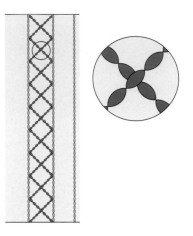

7. In the second segment, draw several stars with chalk, then draw a zigzagging line from a point of each star to the edge of the quilt.

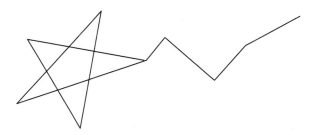

8. Using a walking foot, stitch the diagonal lines, starting at the edge of the quilt, then stitch the star pattern. Pivot at each star point. Tie off the thread tails and bury the ends (see page 48).
9. Change to a darning foot, drop the feed dogs, and double-check that your machine is set for a straight stitch.
10. In the third segment, stitch free-motion meandering curves and loops in several colors. Let the lines cross.
11. Draw another star in chalk, then stitch it free-motion. You can pivot at the points, or better yet, keep the quilt lined up straight and stitch the different angles by moving the quilt in different directions. It helps to pause at each point, then move the quilt evenly. This keeps the ribbon from snagging or twisting on the bobbin-tension hook during stitching.

Threads to Couch

Machine couching is adapted from a hand-embroidery technique. When couching is done by hand, braid is arranged in a looped design on cloth and small spiral stitches are taken around, then under, the arranged braid, attaching it to the fabric. When couching is done by machine, a decorative thread is laid on the quilt surface and simply stitched over with a zigzag or other wide stitch.

Couching can be done on a single layer as a surface embellishment, through two layers—such as a top and a batting—or through all three layers of a quilt sandwich as part of the quilting process. Unlike bobbin quilting, you work right side up. The zigzag or other wide stitch will show on the back of the quilt.

There are several techniques that make couching successful. It's important to know how to secure the decorative work and how to hold and manipulate the braids and yarns. Be sure to read "Couching Basics" on pages 70–73 before beginning the exercise.

Although you can couch decorative thread, braid, cord, ribbon, or yarn, we use the tern *braid* throughout this section for simplicity.

BROADSIDED
by Elizabeth Hendricks. See detail on page 69.

GOLDEN FAIRY by Linda Kallos, 1997, Yellowknife, Northwest Territories, Canada, 25" x 32".
  Free-motion and satin stitched with flat polyester film and with rayon and metallic threads. Couched and beaded.

DETAIL OF SPUN GOLD by Maurine Roy, 1994, Edmonds, Washington, 102" x 102".

Two strands of heavy metallic thread couched along seam lines.

CAMBIA JACKET by Judy Bishop, 1997, Carson, California.

Couched bouclé yarns.

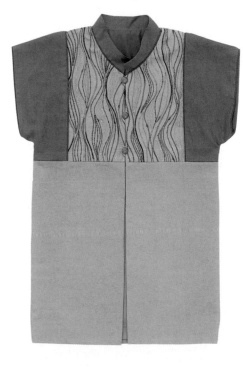

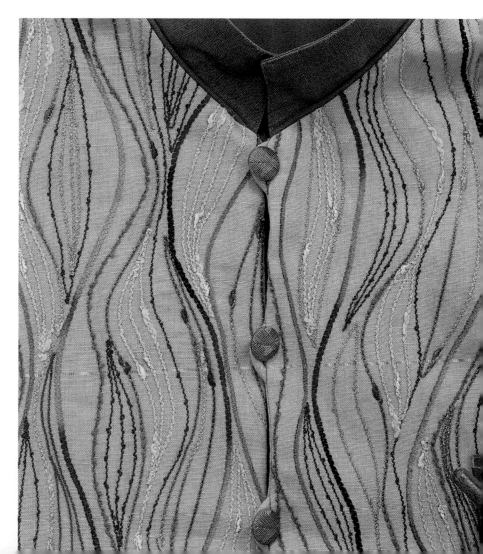

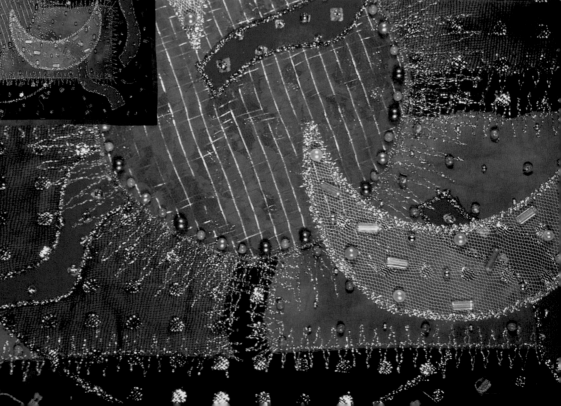

INTIMATE ENCOUNTER
by David Walker, 1997, Cincinnati,
Ohio, 17" x 17".
Couched metallic yarns, braids,
and trims. Netting overlays and
hand beading.

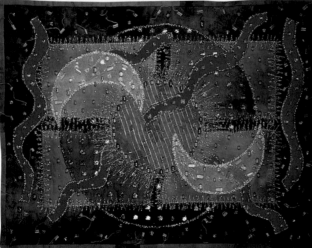

PACIFIC MOONS by David Walker, 1997,
Cincinnati, Ohio, 20" x 15½".
Free-motion stitched with metallic thread
through the needle. Couched threads, yarns, and
braids. Netting overlays and hand beading.

DETAIL OF BROADSIDED
by Elizabeth Hendricks,
1994, Seattle, Washington,
54" x 54".

Free-motion stitched with
variegated rayons and with
metallic and cotton threads.
Couched metallic yarns and
braids. Bobbin quilted with
RibbonFloss.

DETAIL OF CALLIGRAPHY III
by Laura Wasilowski, Elgin,
Illinois, 24" x 19".

Couched hand-dyed #5
pearl cotton.

Couching Basics

$\mathscr{S}$elect a decorative thread to couch. Any of the thicker threads, braids, cords, ribbons, and yarns will work, including those used in bobbin quilting. Many quilting shops carry coordinating yarns and braids on cards. We also venture into weaving, knitting, and needlepoint shops to select interesting yarns and trims.

Choose a top thread. Select a lightweight top thread to use through the needle. The thread can either match or contrast with the fiber content and color of the applied braid. Lightweight metallics; 40-, 50-, and 60-weight rayon; and cotton threads are all appropriate. For example, we like to couch over Kreinik Metallic braid with a metallic thread, and often choose gold to add sparkle. For plied rayons, we select a 40-weight rayon thread that will blend with the applied thread. To couch over a variegated yarn or cord, choose a monofilament thread or a harmonizing cotton thread.

Choose a machine needle. Select a needle appropriate for the top-thread type and weight. Refer to the thread chart on pages 78–80.

Determine the top-thread tension. Loosening the top-thread tension makes it easier to stitch across the bulk of the braid.

Choose a bobbin thread. We prefer polyester or nylon bobbin thread when couching with rayon or metallic threads and cotton thread when couching with cotton.

Set up the braid. It's important to feed the braid so that it doesn't interfere with the top thread or the machine's tension discs. There are several options.

≋ Place the braid in a bowl behind the machine. Bring the braid over the top of the machine, below your thread, and through a guide, such as the handle of the machine.

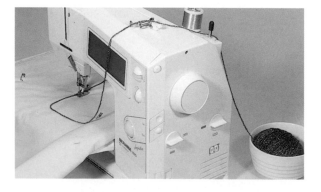

❧ Place the darning foot on the bobbin winder and thread the braid through it.

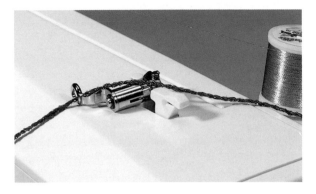

❧ Tape a closed safety pin to the top front of the machine to serve as a guide.

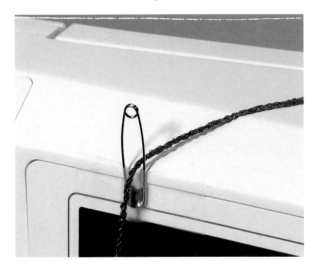

❧ If you're working on a small piece, place the yarn in your lap and let it unroll from there. If you're working on a large piece, this method is impractical because the bulk of the quilt would get in your way.

Select a foot. You can couch with an open-toe foot, a cording/couching foot, or a walking foot. Any foot used for couching must have a groove on the bottom that will accommodate the bulk of the thread, braid, or yarn being couched. Each exercise will specify which foot to use.

❧ The walking foot is great for couching straight lines or gentle curves from one edge to another, or in a pattern with straight sides. The advantage of a walking foot is that it evenly feeds the three layers of the quilt sandwich. This prevents the fabrics from slipping and puckering. The disadvantage of the walking

foot is poor visibility, which is a factor only if you are trying to do intricate geometric designs.

❧ An open-toe foot provides greater visibility. It lets you lay the cording down and secure a key curve or point with a pin, then couch over it without ever lifting the cord. We prefer to use an open-toe foot for intricate patterns and often use it when couching around an appliquéd shape.

❧ The cording/couching foot (also called a braiding foot) has a hole or wire loop in the crosspiece at the front of the foot that accommodates the braid. The advantage of this foot is that the braid feeds through the hole directly in front of the needle, so you need watch only the direction of the foot, not the braid. The disadvantages are limited visibility and the inability to arrange the braid on the fabric first, then stitch over it. We like to use the cording/couching foot for straight lines, which preferably go end to end, and for stitching meandering curves. When turning tight curves with this foot, check the braid as you stitch to make sure it remains centered beneath the stitches.

❧ Multiple-strand foot. There is also a cording/couching foot that handles multiple strands of decorative threads and braids at once. It has a lever that swings open so the threads can be laid in the grooves of the foot with no difficulty. When stitching multiple strands at once, use a stitch wide enough to capture the threads in each stitch. Try a triple-stitch zigzag over the multiple strands or another decorative stitch.

Tip: Thread the cording/couching foot from front to back before placing it on the machine. For limp or fuzzy decorative threads, use a threader.

To create a quick threader, fold a 6" length of strong thread in two. Pinch the fold to make a point, then thread the point through the hole in the foot, from the back toward the front. Keep hold of the threader's ends. Slide the braid through the thread loop, then pull the loop and braid through the hole. Leave a 3" to 4" tail behind the foot as you continue to set up your machine.

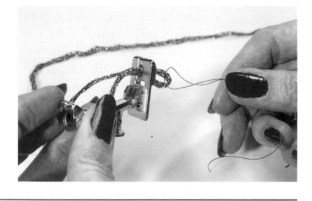

Anchor the stitches. To start couching from the edge of a quilt, lay the cord down with a 2" to 4" tail. Set your machine for a straight stitch. At the quilt's edge, lower the machine needle by hand through the center of the braid, then lower the foot. Take 3 to 5 tiny stitches forward, then the same number of stitches back before beginning to couch.

To begin couching in the center of a piece, or at an intersection, first bury the tail inside the batting. Thread a braid onto a large-eyed hand needle. Pierce the fabric with the hand needle where you want to start couching, then push the needle into the batting nearly flat for 1" to 1½", then out the back. (When using a cording/couching foot, thread the foot first. Then thread a large-eyed hand needle with the tail behind the foot, before piercing the quilt top and burying the tail.)

After taking the hand stitch through the layers, hold the braid as you bring the work forward and under the foot. Make sure the tail doesn't pull out from behind. Take small straight stitches forward and back through the center of the braid where it emerges.

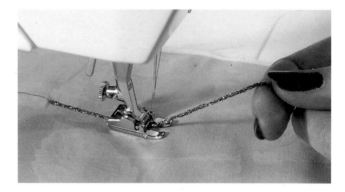

Switch to zigzags. After anchoring the beginning of the braid, change to a zigzag setting. Set the zigzag just a bit wider than the width of your braid. Set the stitch length to approximate the stitch width. For example, if the width is 2.5, set the length to 2.5. Take two to three zigzag stitches over the braid. See that the needle crosses the braid but doesn't pierce it on either side. Adjust the zigzag width and length as needed.

≋ If your machine has decorative stitches, try one in place of the zigzag. Use a contrasting or gold metallic thread to create an interesting pattern.

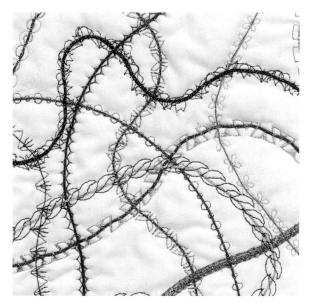

≋ For a unique effect, try stitching a pattern over ribbon. Set the decorative stitch wider than the ribbon.

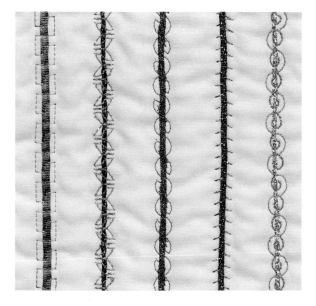

≋ When couching over fluffy threads or chenille yarns, use the blind hem stitch with a monofilament thread. It will hold the yarn or fuzzy thread securely without matting it down, and create an interesting effect.

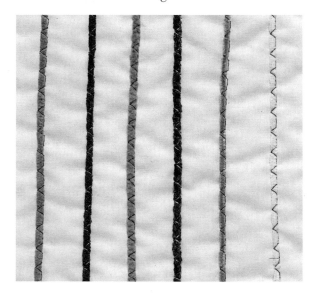

End a line of couching in the center. For couching lines that stop within the quilt and don't extend off the edge, stop the couching stitch 3" to 4" from the end of the design. Leave the machine's needle down in the quilt. Lay the braid down the last few inches in front of the foot, add another 4" of braid, then cut it. Thread the braid on a large-eyed hand needle. Pierce the quilt top where you would like the couching to end, angle the needle nearly flat and toward you through the batting for at least 1", then push needle and braid out the back. Tug gently on the braid, so the braid remaining to be couched on top of the quilt lies flat. Resume couching the braid, then anchor stitch the end.

Tie off thread ends. To finish, thread the top thread on a hand needle and push it straight through to the back. Tie a square knot with the bobbin thread close against the quilt back. Thread both top and bobbin threads onto a hand needle. Angle the needle through the batting about 1", then out the back. Pull the threads taut. Snip off the thread tails where they emerge from the fabric. Pull the braid tail taut and snip it off. The ends should disappear into the quilt. This will keep your work smooth and secure and leave a clean quilt back.

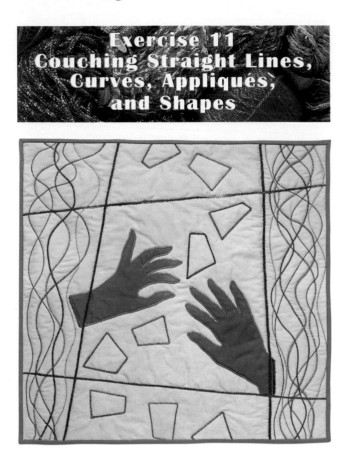

**Exercise 11
Couching Straight Lines,
Curves, Appliqués,
and Shapes**

*Y*ou can couch rayon or metallic braid, thick decorative thread, cording, yarn, and ribbon. Use ribbon only for straight lines or gentle curves.

SETUP CHART	
Couching thread	Braid of your choice
Top thread	40-, 50-, or 60-weight rayon, metallic, cotton or silk thread
Top-thread tension	Slightly loose
Needle	To match top thread
Bobbin thread	To correspond with top thread
Bobbin tension	Normal
Stitch	Straight for anchoring, zigzag for couching
Zigzag length and width	Equal width and length, slightly wider than braid
Speed	Slow to moderate
Foot	Walking, cording/couching, or open-toe; feed dogs up
Quilt position	Backing side down

Preparing to Couch

1. On a 20" square of fabric, draw 2 vertical lines and 2 horizontal lines with chalk to form a box as shown. Your lines can be parallel to the fabric edges or at fun angles. Sandwich the batting and backing; pin baste.

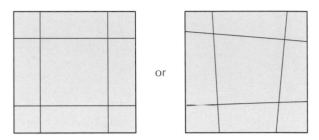

or

2. Using your walking foot, stitch the straight lines edge to edge with cotton thread. Color doesn't matter, since you'll couch over these lines later.

3. On paper, outline your right and left hands. Use the paper patterns to cut each hand from fabric. Pin or fuse them to your quilt.

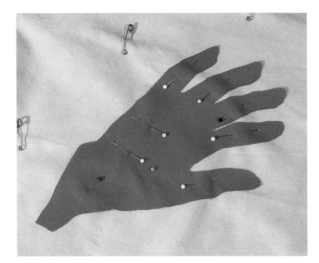

4. Change to an open-toe foot. Using thread to match the fabric, zigzag around each hand. Use a narrow zigzag stitch so the outside stitch just crosses the raw edge. You'll couch around the edges later, after practicing with straight lines and outlined shapes.

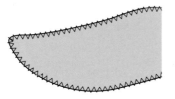

Couching Straight Lines

1. Lay a piece of braid on one of the horizontal or vertical stitched lines, leaving a 2" to 4" tail at the beginning. Do not cut the yarn at the end of the line until the couching is complete.
2. Put a walking foot on the machine. Anchor the beginning of the braid (see page 72). Set the zigzag stitch wider than the braid. Hold the braid in place with your right hand as you stitch to the opposite edge.

3. Anchor stitch the end of the braid. Cut the braid, leaving a 2" to 4" tail.
4. Repeat the process with the other three lines.

Couching Curves

1. Thread a cording/couching foot with braid. Pull a 2" tail behind the foot. Put the foot on the machine.
2. Lower the foot onto the quilt at the end of one of the side borders. Make sure the braid is centered below the needle, then anchor-stitch the braid in place. Set the zigzag stitch wider than the braid.
3. Don't position the braid in front of the foot; the braid will be lifted up and through the foot as you stitch. Instead, with both hands on the quilt, simply turn the quilt gently to the right, then to the left as you zigzag stitch. This motion will form graceful curved lines.

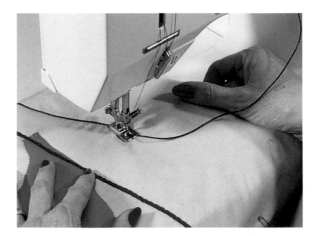

4. Repeat the process with other colors and types of braids. Allow the curves to cross previously stitched lines.

Note: You can also use an open-toe foot when stitching curves. However, it's necessary to hold the braid in position with one hand while turning the quilt with the other.

Outlining Shapes

1. With chalk, draw geometric shapes in the center of the box.
2. Thread your braid through a large-eyed hand needle. Select a point on your shape and pierce the top of the quilt. Run the needle through the batting for 1" to 1½". Pull the braid through, leaving a 2" tail on the back.

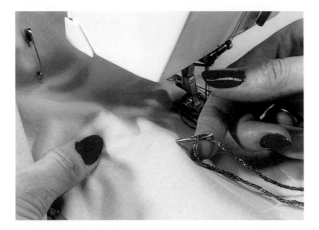

3. Put on an open-toe foot for better visibility. Lower the machine needle by hand to pierce the braid where it emerges from the quilt top. Anchor the stitches. Set the zigzag stitch wider than the braid and stitch to the first corner of the shape.
4. Stop with the needle down, inside a corner. Raise the foot, and pivot the quilt to line up with the next side of the shape. Stitch to the next corner and repeat.

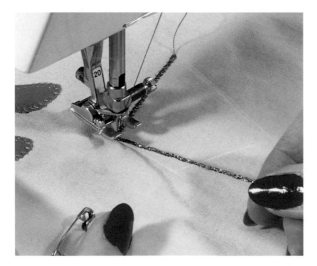

5. Stop before stitching the final side of the design. Lay the braid down on the last side and cut it off, leaving a 4" tail. Thread the braid on a large-eyed hand needle and pierce the quilt at the last corner. Once again, run the needle through the batting for 1" to 1½", then out the back. Remove the braid from the needle, and pull it taut from behind.
6. Zigzag the final side. Anchor stitch at the corner to secure the braid.

7. Pull the top thread to the back. Tie the thread tails in a square knot. Thread the tails on a large-eyed hand needle and run the tails through the batting. Pull the braid and thread tails taut, then cut them off.
8. Repeat this process for additional geometric shapes.

Couching Raw-Edge Appliqué

1. To couch around the hands you appliquéd at the beginning of this exercise, thread the braid on a large-eyed hand needle. Pierce the quilt under the couched yarn edge of the box where the shape emerges.
2. Run the needle through the batting and out the back, leaving a 4" tail.

3. Put on an open-toe embroidery foot. Center the braid over the raw edge of the shape. Anchor stitch, then begin the zigzag stitch. Hold the quilt steady with your left hand as you hold the braid in front of the foot with your right hand. Try to keep the braid centered over the raw edge as you stitch.

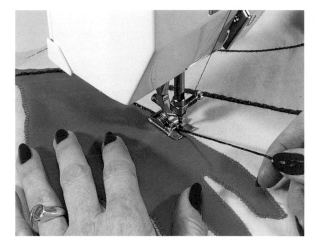

≋ To stitch around a curve, hold the braid with your right hand so it follows the curve, while your left hand turns the quilt.
≋ For points, pivot with the needle down on the inside of the turn.

≋ If you want to add a second row of couching next to the first, choose a braid or decorative thread smaller than the first one. A second row gives shapes dimension and adds a nice finish.

After you have completed the couching, you may wish to free-motion quilt the background fabric with cotton, rayon, or metallic thread to complete the stitching on your small quilt.

NEEDLES

All needles are by Schmetz unless otherwise noted.

Type	Size	Description
SHARP NEEDLES WITH NORMAL-SIZE EYES		
Sharp Microtex	60/8 to 90/14	Extra-sharp point for perfectly straight stitches, topstitching, or edgestitching; works well with microfibers
Jeans/Denim	70/10 to 110/18	Sharp point for densely woven fabrics
Quilting	75/11 & 90/14	Special taper to point for penetrating multiple layers (quilt top and seam allowances)
SHARP NEEDLES WITH LARGER-THAN-NORMAL EYES		
Embroidery Madeira Embroidery	75/11, 80/12, & 90/14	Larger eye and deeper scarf prevents rayon and some metallic threads from shreading and breaking
Metallica, Metafil (Lammertz) Madeira Metallic	70/10, 80/12 or 90/14	Larger eye than Embroidery needle; made to prevent stripping and fraying of metallic threads
Topstitch (System 130N)	80/12 to 110/20	Extra-large eye and scarf accommodate heavy and textured threads
Twin Embroidery	2.0/75–3.0/75	For rayon or embroidery threads; makes 2 rows of stitching
Twin Metallica	2.0/80–3.0/80	For metallic threads; makes 2 rows of stitching

THREADS TO STITCH THROUGH THE NEEDLE

Brand Name	Fiber Content	Weight	Suggested Needles	Description
INVISIBLE OR MONOFILAMENT *Use same thread or lightweight cotton in bobbin. All brands are available in clear and smoke.*				
Madeira Monofil Sulky Invisible	Polyester	.004 mm	Sharp or Denim 70/10 or 80/12; Quilting 75/11	Lightweight, soft, and pliable
Sew-Art YLI Wonder	Nylon	.004mm	Sharp or Denim 70/10 or 80/12; Quilting 75/11	Lightweight, soft, and pliable
LIGHTWEIGHT COTTON: *Use same thread in bobbin.*				
DMC 50	Cotton	100	Sharp or Denim 70/10 or 80/12; Quilting 75/11	Lightweight machine embroidery thread; good for dense quilting and satin stitching
Madeira Cotona	Cotton	80 & 50	Sharp or Denim 70/10 or 80/12; Quilting 75/11	80 is very lightweight, 50 heavier than DMC; good for dense quilting
Mettler Embroidery	Cotton	60/2	Sharp or Denim 70/10 or 80/12; Quilting 75/11	Heavier than Cotona 80 or DMC 50; good for dense quilting and bobbin thread
Mettler Silk Finish	Cotton	50/3	Sharp or Denim 80/12, or Quilting 75/11	Stronger, heavier, good for piecing and anchor quilting
Coats Dual Duty Machine Embroidery	Cotton-polyester		Sharp or Denim 80/12, or Quilting 75/11	Finer than Coats regular Dual Duty
Coats Mercerized Gütermann Cotton	Cotton	50	Sharp or Denim 80/12, or Quilting 75/11	Heavier than Silk Finish; good for piecing and anchor quilting

THREADS TO STITCH THROUGH THE NEEDLE (CONTINUED)

Brand Name	Fiber Content	Weight	Suggested Needles	Description
HEAVYWEIGHT THREADS: *Use same thread or 30-weight cotton in bobbin.*				
Madeira Cotona Madeira Tanne Mettler Machine Emb.	Cotton	30	Sharp or Denim 90/14, or Quilting 90/14	Heavy machine embroidery thread; Mettler available in variegated colors
Mettler Cordonnet YLI Jeanstitch Gütermann Topstitch	Polyester	30/3	Topstitch 90/14	Heavyweight topstitching thread, solid colors; sashiko look
Gütermann Silk Topstitch	Silk		Topstitch 90/14 or 100/16	Similar to above, shreds more easily
Mettler Quilting	Cotton	40/3	Quilting 90/14 or Topstitch 80/12	Stitches an attractive solid ine
Gunold Stickma Cotty Artfabrik Pearl Cotton DMC Pearl Cotton Anchor Pearl Cotton Caron Wildflower	Cotton	#12	Embroidery 90/14 or Topstitch 80/12	Lightest-weight pearl cotton. Artfabrik and Caron Wildflowers available in hand-dyed and variegated colors.
DMC Pearl Cotton Artfabrik Pearl Cotton Anchor Pearl Cotton	Cotton	#8	Topstitch 100/16	Heavyweight pearl cotton; tighten top tension; easier to use in bobbin. Artfabrik available in hand-dyed variegated colors.
Sew-Art Renaissance Madeira Burmilana Gunold Stickma Luny	30% wool/ 70% acrylic		Topstitch 90/14 or 100/16	Woolly yarn; looks like crewel embroidery thread
RAYON THREAD: *Use same thread, bobbin thread, or 60-weight cotton in bobbin.*				
Madeira Rayon Sulky Rayon Coats Rayon	Rayon	40 & 30	Embroidery 75/11 or 90/14	40-wt. solid, variegated and ombré colors; 30-wt. solids. Madeira 30-wt. variegated looks hand painted
Coats Color Twist Rayon	Rayon	35	Embroidery 75/11 or 90/14	2 colors twisted together, heathery look; also variegated
Signature Rayon Gütermann Rayon Sew-Art Rayon	Rayon	40	Embroidery 75/11 or 90/14	Solids and variegated
Madeira Neon	Polyester	40	Embroidery 75/11 or 90/14	Showy fluorescent
Gütermann Silk Kanagawa Silk Tire Silk YLI Silk	Silk	50	Embroidery 75/11 or 90/14	Elegant luster, strong
YLI Heirloom	Silk	100	Embroidery 75/11	Very lightwieght; lustrous and strong

THREADS TO STITCH THROUGH THE NEEDLE (CONTINUED)

Brand Name	Fiber Content	Weight	Suggested Needles	Description
LIGHTWEIGHT METALLIC THREADS: *Use polyester or nylon bobbin thread.*				
Smooth Metallics				
Gütermann Metallic Kreinik #1 Japan Thread Kreinik Cord Madeira Metallic Mettler Metallic Sew-Art Metallic Signature Metallic Sulky Metallic YLI Fine Metallic	Metallic polyester	Varies	Embroidery 90/14 or Metallic 70/10, 80/12, or 90/14	Smooth, fine; solids and variegated
Madeira FS2/2 Jewel (also called Blackcore)	Metallic polyester	40	Metallic 80/12	Smooth, blend of twisted black and colored metallic, some variegated
Textured Metallics				
Coats Metallic Madeira Metallic Madeira Supertwist	Metallic polyester	40	Metallic 80/12 or 90/14 or Topstitch 90/14	Rough texture, blend of sparkly and iridescent fibers; some two-color twists. Loosen top tension.
Multi-strand Metallics				
Mettler Heavy Metal Gütermann Metallic DMC Metallic Madeira #15 Metallic	Metallic polyester	Varies	Metallic 90/14 or Topstitch 90/14	Heavy, rich appearance. Limited colors. Free-motion stitch with care; may be more successful in bobbin.
FLAT, RIBBONLIKE POLYESTER FILM: *Use polyester or nylon bobbin thread.*				
Sulky Sliver Coats Glitz	Polyester		Embroidery 90/14 or Metallic 70/10, 80/12, or 90/14	Reflective; many colors
Madeira Jewel Glissen Gloss Prizm Hologram	Polyester		Embroidery 90/14 or Metallic 70/10, 80/12, or 90/14	Reflective, faceted, sparkly hologram look

BOBBIN THREADS FOR LIGHTWEIGHT TOP THREADS

Brand Name	Fiber Content	Color	Suggested Top Thread	Description
YLI Lingerie & Bobbin Sew-Art/Sew Bob	Nylon	Black & White	Good with lightweight metallics, rayon, cotton or monofilament	Very lightweight, but smooth and strong. Slightly stretchy; soft and supple.
Madeira Bobbinfil Sulky Bobbin Mettler Metrolene	Polyester			Metrolene available in 12 additional colors.

THREADS TO STITCH FROM THE BOBBIN OR TO COUCH

Brand Name	Fiber Content	Weight	Suggested Top Thread	Description/Uses
PLIED THREADS: *All can be bobbin quilted with a walking foot or couched.*				
Madeira Decor YLI Designer 6 Sew-Art Floss 6	Rayon	No. 6	Rayon	Multiple strands of fine plied (untwisted) rayon. Very soft, with beautiful sheen. Best stitched in straight lines or gentle curves with a walking foot. Free-motion stitch with care.
DMC or Madeira Embroidery Floss	Silk or cotton	6 strands	Silk or rayon	To bobbin quilt, handle 6 strands as 1. Same tolerance as Decor
PEARL THREADS: *All can be bobbin quilted with a walking foot or couched.*				
YLI Pearl Crown Rayon Sew-Art Pearl Crown Rayon	Rayon	Heavy	Rayon	Rich, lustrous sheen. Well-suited to complex designs. Recommend highly for free-motion stitching.
DMC Pearl Cotton Anchor Pearl Cotton Artfabrik Pearl Cotton	Cotton	#3, #5, & #8	50-wt. cotton	Matte to soft luster, tightly twisted. Lightest weight, #8, can be used on top with a 100/16 Topstitch needle. All weights great for bobbin quilting free motion.
ROUND BRAIDS: *All can be bobbin quilted with a walking foot or couched.*				
Kreinik	Metallic polyester	#4 very fine metallic #8 fine #12 tapestry #16 medium		Glimmering metallic. Both fine and medium weights can be bobbin quilted. Stitches tight curves and complex designs well. Recommend highly for free-motion stitching.
METALLIC THREADS: *All can be bobbin quilted with a walking foot or couched.*				
Sew-Art Symphony	Acrylic-metallic blend	Heavy	Smooth metallic	Soft, with fuzzy matte look. Easiest to stitch in straight lines or gentle curves.
YLI Candlelight	Rayon & metallic polyester	No. 8	Smooth metallic	Free-motion stitch with care.
Sew-Art Flash	Rayon & metallic	Heavy	Smooth metallic	Rough, lustrous. Wind flat in the bobbin like ribbon to avoid twisting.
Madeira Metallic #6	Viscose & metallic polyester	No. 6	Smooth metallic	Beautiful round, smooth thread in gold and silver. Easy to handle. Stitches smoothly. Recommend highly for free motion.
Madeira Glamour	Viscose & polyester	No. 8	Smooth metallic	Soft, nubbly, heavyweight. Beautiful bold line. Easy to handle. Each stitch scallops slightly. Recommend highly for free motion.
DMC Metallic Embroidery Floss	Viscose & metallic polyester	6-strand	Smooth metallic	Treat the 6 strands as one when loading the bobbin. Can snag or tangle on bobbin tension disc, so free-motion stitch only gentle curves and use care.
Kreinik Ombre	Polyester & viscose metallic	Medium	Smooth metallic	8 lightly twisted filaments; supple, with soft, sparkly look. Stitches smoothly. Great on tight curves. Recommend highly for free motion.
Kreinik Japan Thread	Silver metallic w/ paper base on nylon core	#1, #5, & #7	Smooth metallic	Gorgeous smooth, round, wiry thread. Stitches beautifully. Best with short stitches. Great on tight curves; can buckle on sharp points. Recommend highly for free motion.

THREADS TO STITCH FROM THE BOBBIN OR TO COUCH (CONTINUED)

Brand Name	Fiber Content	Weight	Suggested Top Thread	Description/Uses
Madeira Metallic	Polyester & metallic	Varies	Smooth metallic	Embroidery threads ranging from soft metallics to stiff, wiry threads. Versatility varies.
Kreinik Cable	Polyester viscose & nylon core	Fine	Smooth metallic	A 3-ply twisted cord. Fine and wiry. Glides easily through bobbin. So stiff it rounds sharp points. Free-motion stitch with care.
Kreinik Blending Filament	Polyester & viscose or nylon	Very fine	Smooth metallic	Fine and delicate with a slight twist. Three kinds: basic, high luster, and glow-in-the-dark. Top-thread tension normal. Recommend highly for tight designs. Can be bobbin wound in multiple strands or with other threads.
True Colors Pre-blended Thread, high luster	Polyester & nylon	No. 14	Metallic	Soft and sparkly; long filaments. Tighten bobbin tension slightly and loosen top-thread tension to normal. Free-motion stitch with care.
FLAT BRAIDS: *All can be bobbin quilted with a walking foot or couched.*				
Madeira Metallic Braid	Metallic polyester	No. 8	Metallic	Subtle blend of silver and gold; sparkly. Good with large programmed zigzags. Not recommended for free-motion stitching.
Kreinik Braid	Polyester viscose	No. 4	Metallic	Made of 4 strands of blending filament. Can be high luster, or solid or blended colors. High luster is flattest.
RIBBONS: *Free-motion stitch with care. Great with a walking foot.* *Ribbons can also be couched with zigzag or wide decorative stitches.*				
Rayon RibbonFloss	Rayon		Rayon	Lustrous, supple, flat ribbon.
Shimmer Blend RibbonFloss	Rayon w/ metallic strand		Rayon or metallic	Supple, flat ribbon with metallic thread running throughout.
Metallic RibbonFloss	Metallic		Strong metallic	Soft, reflective ribbon. Increase top tension for scalloped stitch.
Neon Rays Needlepoint Ribbon	Rayon		Rayon	Supple ribbon with pretty sheen. Iron flat before winding on bobbin.
Frye Werks Metallic Ribbon	Polyester & nylon		Strong metallic	Sparkly, highly reflective, soft metallic ribbon. Stitches free-motion with ease. Iron flat before winding onto bobbin.
YLI Silk Ribbon Alaska DyeWorks Silk Ribbon	Silk		Silk or rayon	Smooth ribbon in sumptuous colors. 2mm-wide ribbon free-motion stitches beautifully. 4mm needs longer stitch; tends to bunch at corners. Stitch free-motion with care.
Kreinik Metallic Ribbon	Polyester Metallic		Metallic or rayon	Soft ribbon. Stitches beautifully. Use long stitch. Both 1/16" and 1/8" width.

THREADS TO STITCH FROM THE BOBBIN OR TO COUCH (CONTINUED)

Brand Name/ Category	Fiber	Weight Content	Suggested Top Thread	Description/Uses
YARNS FOR COUCHING				
Metallic Yarns	Metallic & blends	Heavy	Metallic	Appearance and handling varies with different yarns. Couches beautifully.
Chenille	Cotton	Heavy	Cotton or rayon	Untwist and lay flat for couching. Retains body with blind hem stitch. Look for fabulous hand-dyed.
Rainbow Gallery Razzle-Dazzle 6	Nylon & polyester	No. 6	Metallic	Rough, sparkly metallic. Couches curves well.
Quilter's Resource Radiance	Rayon & lurex	Heavy	Metallic	Reflective, rough. Bright sparkle when couched.
Quilter's Resource Bouclé	Rayon & cotton	Heavy	Metallic or Rayon	Twisted, delightfully uneven. Creates an interesting line. Many variegated colors.
Madeira Lurana	Viscose & metallic	No. 3	Metallic	Soft, shiny, or glittery mixed colors.
Madeira Acrylana	Acrylic	No. 4	Rayon or metallic	Soft, slightly fuzzy yarn. Some have gold threads running throughout.
Madeira Viscona No. 2	Rayon	No. 2	Rayon	Round braid with a soft sheen
Caron Double-Dipped Rachel	Nylon	Tubular	Rayon or metallic	Soft, tubular nylon; has gauzelike appearance. Attractive in wide programmed stitches.
Caron Waterlilies	Silk	12-ply	Silk or rayon	Soft, luscious hand-painted silk. Handles curves well.
Caron Watercolors	Pima cotton	3-ply	Rayon or cotton	Soft, luminous hand-painted braid. Variegated color.
HEAVY BRAIDS FOR COUCHING				
Kreinik Heavy Braid	Polyester & metallic	#32 Heavy	Metallic	Round metallic. Couches well in curves and angled designs. Lighter weight can be couched for fine lines.
Madeira Carat	Metallic & nylon	2mm & 4mm	Metallic	Flat, shimmery metallic. Couches beautifully. Try decorative stitch. Best couched in straight lines.
Rainbow Gallery Gold Rush 12	Metallized polyester & viscose	No. 12	Metallic	Soft; couches beautifully on curves.
OTHER GOODIES TO COUCH				
String of sequins			Metallic or monofilament	Zigzag strands, then tug strand down to make the stitches slip under the sequins. Easiest to handle in straight lines.
String of pearls	Faux pearls		Rayon, metallic, or monofilament	Couch with a foot that allows the pearls to pass under a groove on foot.
Kreinik Facet	Polyester & viscose		Metallic or rayon	One cord wrapped around another to give beadlike look. Very sparkly.

Resources

Alaska Dyeworks
300 West Swanson, Suite #101
Wasilla, AK 99654
1-800-478-1755
hand-dyed fabrics and silk ribbon

Artfabrik
324 Vincent Place
Elgin, IL 60123
(847) 931-7684
*hand-dyed variegated pearl
cotton threads, and fabrics*

Creative Stitches
230 West 1700 South
Salt Lake City, UT 84115
(800) 748-5144
thread, stabilizers

Daisy Chain
PO Box 1258
Parkersburg, WV 26102
(800) 311-8061
thread, yarn

DARR, Inc.
2370-G Hillcrest Road #121
Mobile, AL 36695
EZ Winder

Design and Sew Patterns
Lois Erickson
Box 5222
Salem, OR 97304
wearable-art clothing patterns

Judy Bishop Designs
24603 Island Avenue
Carson, CA 90745
wearable art clothing patterns

Nordic Needle
1314 Gateway Drive
Fargo, ND 58103
(800) 433-4321
thread

Sew-Art International
PO Box 1244
Bountiful, UT 84011
(800) 231-2787
thread, stabilizers

SoftWear Productions
2523 S. Archer Avenue
Chicago, IL 60608-5911
(800) 297-9670
sewing supplies, thread

Sophisticated Stitchery
PO Box 263
Carteret, NJ 07008
(800) 669-0408
thread, yarn

Speed Stitch (Sulky)
3113-D Broadpoint Drive
Harbor Heights, FL 33983
(800) 874-4115
Sulky products

Web of Thread
1410 Broadway
Paducah, KY 42001
(800) 955-8185
specialty threads, ribbons

Templates

Start

Centerline

Trace the heart half onto tracing
paper. Flip the tracing paper
over, match the center lines, and
trace the other half of the heart.
If you can't see the first half
clearly through the paper, trace
it onto the front.